Endorsements

Fearless: Ordinary Women of the Bible who Dared to do Extraordinary Things is an inspiring discovery of what happens when uncommon faith and unstoppable courage are empowered by the Spirit. Scripture has proven it and the church reflects it, that the kingdom of God is advanced with greater effectiveness when God-gifted and called daughters are engaged in ministry and leadership. Caution! Reading this book may cause you to realize some God sized dreams for your life.

—REV. DOUG CLAY, Chairman, World Assemblies of God Fellowship

She's done it again—Angela Donadio has written a wonderful book! Her biblical exegesis is deep and captivating—she's definitely done her homework on the texts. Yet while she is immersed in the ancient texts and languages, she speaks to a contemporary audience touching on our issues in today's language. The six fearless women she spotlights, though ordinary, are exemplary—terrific models for us all. I am inspired and challenged (and can't wait for Angela's next book).

—DEBORAH M. GILL, Ph.D., Professor, Biblical Studies and Exposition Chair, Bible and Theology Department and Masters Programs, Assemblies of God Theological Seminary, Evangel University

Angela Donadio and I are alike in many ways—we are both committed to the Word of God, to ministering to women and we both have been married for many years to a pastor. However, Angela is something that I am not—she is an adventurer to the very core of her being. I don't have one adventurous cell in my body! While Angela climbs mountains—I read books. While Angela lives in jungle huts—I enjoy 4-star resorts.

I must tell you—that even though I am not adventurous that I am indeed, fearless just like my friend, Angela. As I read her new book, I was challenged to live with reckless abandon for the Kingdom of God. I was dared, once again, to be wholehearted in my commitment to Christ and His Kingdom. I purposed, after reading Angela's new book, to have the same divine impact that women like Rahab, Priscilla and Abigail had at their moment in history. Let's do this! Let's be fearless as we serve the God of miracles!

—CAROL MCLEOD, Best-selling Author and Bible Teacher, Radio Host and Blogger, Author of 11 books including, *Joy for All Seasons*

This book is a masterpiece. Angela, herself is both a New Testament and a 21st century example of a fearless woman of God, accomplishing great things for God in the USA, Africa and other parts of the world. She reveals how some women in the Bible exhibited greater courage than men, confirming the scripture which says," God is no respecter of persons" and demonstrating that God can use anybody. This book will turn many lives into useful vessels in the hands of God.

—DR. STEPHEN Y WENGAM, Lead Pastor, Cedar Mountain Chapel, East Legon-Accra, Ghana, West Africa/Resident Radio Pastor, Citi 97.3fm

---

Angela is not only a Bible teacher, but a friend who knows what it's like to live with fear and beyond it. She guides us through several stories of women in the Bible who had every right to be afraid. But the truth Angela shows us is how to live a fearless life of faith. You will be challenged and encouraged through this simple, yet deep study of women of the Bible. Angela traveled to Israel and gives us insight directly from the real-life location of some of these stories. You will be inspired to let go of the fear that is holding you back.

—MICAH MADDOX, National Women's Conference Speaker and Author of *Anchored In: Experience a Power-Full Life in a Problem-Filled World*

Dedication

To Dale, my husband and partner for life. Thank you for reading every word and inspiring me to find my fearless. To Gabrielle and Christian, my children and now, my friends. Thank you for cheering me on and loving me through every adventure. I love my tribe. You're amazing and I could never do this without you. To every woman who holds this book in your hands: stand up, stand out, and stand strong as you find your fearless in Christ.

Acknowledgements

Thank you, Jesus. You know me better than anyone else and love me best. You continually guide me to find my fearless in You. Thank you, Dale. Your love steadies me through every adventure. I love doing life with you. None of this would be the same without you. Thank you, Gabrielle and Christian. You've taken this journey with me and I'm forever grateful. No matter what happens in life, keep your compass pointed north to Jesus. Thank you, Mom and Dad. You invested your time, energy, love, resources, and most of all—Jesus—into my life. Watching you weather life's challenges framed the way I view my own. This labor of love became even more special with my Dad's input. I'm forever grateful.

Thank you to extended family and family in heaven. Your legacy continues to inspire generations to find their fearless in Christ. Thank you, River of Life Family. You've had a front row seat to every dark valley and steep mountain climb. You've carried me through seasons of unbelievable difficulty and unbridled joy with open arms. I'm truly blessed.

Thank you, my "Fearless" tribe of women who dreamt with me and played a critical role in this project. Deanna Ragsdale, Sabrina Gurney, Miriam Stocks, Anita McDermott, Cathy Woehrle, Kim Bohn, and Denise Johnson, thank you for brainstorming with me and supporting me every step of the way. Ruth Donadio, Stacey Martin, Lauren Gerhard, Izla Hearn and Janet Swink, thank you for reading every word and pushing me over the finish line.

Thank you to those who graciously extended your endorsement of this book. I admire your leadership and unwavering faith more than you'll ever know. Thank you, Jim Hart at Hartline Agency. Your guidance as my agent has been invaluable. You've helped me to stay true to my convictions and pursue my calling. Thank you, Suzi Wooldridge and the Bridge Logos Family. I'm over the moon to take this journey with you and look forward to future endeavors.

Contents

Introduction

Welcome to *"Fearless: Ordinary Women of the Bible who Dared to do Extraordinary Things."* When the concept for *"Fearless"* was in its infancy, I had all kinds of ideas about how it might turn out. Girls—these women exceeded every expectation. I knew I wanted to cover some of the *"Best Supporting Actresses"* of the Bible—women we knew less about than some of their contemporaries. My early research contributed a loose framework around their list of accomplishments but provided only a glimpse into their personalities. The more I studied, the more I discovered about the unique challenges they faced. The more I prayed, the more I received insight from the Holy Spirit about the distinct role they played. I poured over historical records of each time period and examined countless commentaries and theological perspectives. I filled notebooks to the brim with descriptors and details. And something became abundantly clear: *there was nothing ordinary about these women.*

In the pages of this resource, part study—part story, you'll meet fearless women who dared to do extraordinary things because they grounded themselves in the Word instead of the world. They show us how to stand up in uncommon ways for the common good. They display what it looks like to stand out with confidence in a fog of uncertainty. They demonstrate what it looks like to stand strong as a source of immeasurable value to the kingdom of God. And we, beautiful women, can find our fearless in their stories.

This resource contains six Sessions, designed for individual or group study. Each session provides four "Find Your Fearless" response sections, with key takeaways, thought-provoking questions, a fearless declaration, and an opportunity to write a prayer in your own words. These questions offer ideal talking points for group study.

To receive the maximum benefit of this resource, use the link or QR code provided before each Introduction to view the corresponding video. Filmed in Israel, these videos will enhance your study and deepen your understanding of the women you're studying. I'm praying for you as you find your fearless in their stories.

I'd love to connect with you! Join my email community at www. angeladonadio.com, and like and follow me on social media. Find me on Facebook at angeladonadiovov, and Instagram at angeladonadio. Post your favorite quotes on social media using #findyourfearless. For booking inquiries, please email angela@angeladonadio.com or www. angeladonadio.com.

The Women Who Delivered a Deliverer

Their Story & Our Starting Place

> God can preserve our hope.

EXODUS 1:15—2:10

Before you begin your study, view the companion video resource here:

www.angeladonadio.com

I have also included the video message and our key Scripture passage below.

Welcome to *Fearless!* These aren't just ancient stories about women of the Bible. They're our sisters...our girlfriends...our moms. For our first session, we're journeying thousands of years into the past to read about not one, but several women who stood up to the injustice of their culture and helped deliver a deliverer: Moses. You'll meet the fearless heroines in this story, each willing to play their part so God could preserve hope.

The midwives, Shiphrah and Puah, show us the *providence* of God.

Jochebed, mother of Aaron, Moses, and Miriam, shows us the *preservation* of God.

And two daughters, Miriam, the daughter of Jochebed, and the unnamed daughter of Pharaoh, point us to the *provision* of God.

Moses was born at a volatile time in Israel's history, during the 18th Egyptian dynasty, 1500 years before the birth of Jesus Christ, the Messiah. The people of Israel, enslaved for 400 years, faced cruel oppression under the tyrannical rule of the Pharaohs. The Book of Acts records this tremendously troubled time in a speech delivered by Stephen to the religious leaders just moments before he was martyred for his faith in Christ.

Acts 7:17: "As the time drew near for God to fulfill His promise to Abraham, the number of our people in Egypt greatly increased. Then another king, who knew nothing about Joseph, became ruler of Egypt. He dealt treacherously with our people and oppressed our forefathers by forcing them to throw out their newborn baby boys, so they would die."

Against this brutal backdrop, Jochebed found herself pregnant. What should've been one of the most joyous times in a woman's life was instead filled with terror. Faced with uncertainty and trapped by a culture in crisis, Jochebed dared to believe that God was in control.

Hebrews 11:23 gives us powerful insight into her state of mind: "By faith Moses' parents hid him for three months after he was born because they saw he was no ordinary child, and they were not afraid of the king's edict."

Jochebed stood up against oppression, fearlessly placing her trust in God. Women, God can preserve our hope. Come with me to the Holy Land!

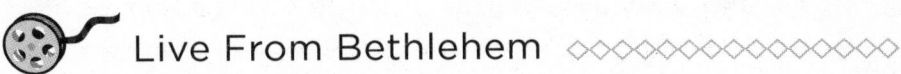 Live From Bethlehem

I'm standing in one of my favorite places in all of Israel: Bethlehem. Who would dream that the provision to preserve the hope of all mankind would come from here—a feeding trough in a dark, damp cave? But this is the place where Jesus was born. Who would've thought that 1500 years earlier, provision would come from a hand-crafted cradle coated with tar? In Exodus, we read the story of the women who delivered a deliverer. These women summoned the courage to resist the will of Egypt's all powerful, sovereign leader, at the risk of their own lives.

Let's read their story in Exodus 1:15–2:10.

> "The king of Egypt said to the Hebrew midwives, whose names were Shiphrah and Puah, "When you are helping the Hebrew women during childbirth on the delivery stool, if you see that the baby is a boy, kill him; but if it is a girl, let her live." The midwives, however, feared God and did not do what the king of Egypt had told them to do; they let the boys live. Then the king of Egypt summoned the midwives and asked them, "Why have you done this? Why have you let the boys live?"
>
> The midwives answered Pharaoh, "Hebrew women are not like Egyptian women; they are vigorous and give birth before the midwives arrive."
>
> So God was kind to the midwives and the people increased and became even more numerous. And because the midwives feared God, he gave them families of their own.
>
> Then Pharaoh gave this order to all his people: "Every Hebrew boy that is born you must throw into the Nile, but let every girl live."

> Now a man of the tribe of Levi married a Levite woman, and she became pregnant and gave birth to a son. When she saw that he was a fine child, she hid him for three months. But when she could hide him no longer, she got a papyrus basket for him and coated it with tar and pitch. Then she placed the child in it and put it among the reeds along the bank of the Nile. His sister stood at a distance to see what would happen to him.
>
> Then Pharaoh's daughter went down to the Nile to bathe, and her attendants were walking along the riverbank. She saw the basket among the reeds and sent her female slave to get it. She opened it and saw the baby. He was crying, and she felt sorry for him. "This is one of the Hebrew babies," she said.
>
> Then his sister asked Pharaoh's daughter, "Shall I go and get one of the Hebrew women to nurse the baby for you?"
>
> "Yes, go," she answered. So the girl went and got the baby's mother. Pharaoh's daughter said to her, "Take this baby and nurse him for me, and I will pay you." So the woman took the baby and nursed him. When the child grew older, she took him to Pharaoh's daughter and he became her son. She named him Moses, saying, "I drew him out of the water."

I can't imagine what it must have felt like for Moses' mother to put her 3-month-old baby in a basket and place him in the Nile. Or what it must have been like for the mother of Jesus to give birth to our hope in this place. These women lived ordinary lives but dared to do extraordinary things because they put their faith in God. Girls, our ordinary, everyday moments can become platforms for the miraculous when we choose obedience and place our trust in God.

◇◇◇

Looking out over the shepherds' fields in Bethlehem, one word kept resonating in my spirit: hope. It was here that David patiently tended sheep until God anointed him for divine purpose. It was here that shepherds carefully guarded their flocks until God announced the birth of a Savior through angelic messengers. And, it was here that a young girl named Mary delivered a baby in a nearby cave. In seemingly ordinary moments, or just when things seem the darkest, God breathes hope.

Mary placed her hope in a feeding trough in Bethlehem, just as thousands of years earlier, Jochebed placed her hope in a papyrus basket in Egypt. But these fearless women truly placed their hope in God. As Jochebed set Moses in the Nile, the enemy's tool for destruction became God's instrument for preservation.

Our ordinary moments become extraordinary when we put our hope in the Lord. Perhaps you're walking through a season of uncertainty with more questions than answers. As we study the women who delivered a deliverer, trust that God has the final say in your situation. These fearless women will help us discover this important truth: God can preserve our hope.

God can PRESERVE our hope.

Her Cause—Stand Up

THE MIDWIVES

The sun glistened as it danced on the Nile River. Reeds blew gently in the wind, naive to the palpable pain thickening the air. Choking back quiet sobs, Jochebed clutched him next to her heart until she thought it might break. Her hands still sticky from tar, she placed him into the basket she had woven for this moment.

As her feet slipped into the muddy marsh, hot tears slid down her face. She pushed back the "what-if" thoughts threatening to steal her resolve and looked one last time into her child's trusting eyes.

"I know something is different about you. I know Jehovah has destined you for greatness. I don't understand everything that is happening right now, or why I have to say goodbye to you, but I know that He will protect you and protect our people. Every time I brushed this basket with tar, I whispered a prayer over you. I love you and I'm letting you go so Jehovah can take care of you."

With that, Jochebed stepped back and held her breath. She felt secure that the cradle of plaited papyrus reeds she meticulously wove together was watertight. She was confident that Pharaoh's daughter would come to bathe at any minute. Yet her faith didn't lie in a tiny basket or even in the compassion of the daughter of royalty. Her trust was in God.

Picture for a moment what it might have been like for Jochebed to crouch in the weeds and wait. Did she fully understand the ways her actions would affect generations to come? How could she have known her child would become one of the greatest leaders of the Old Testament? Just as a relay race requires members of a team to take turns passing a baton as they complete their leg of the race, God's means for salvation required several women to carry their baton with faith. Midwives, Jochebed, Miriam, and Pharaoh's daughter, all ran their portion of a divinely-orchestrated race. Their obedience constituted far more than crossing a finish line: it determined the course of history. Just who was this deliverer they helped deliver?

"Moses was the instrument through which Israel experienced salvation. The Exodus—the experience of the Jewish people being led from slavery in Egypt to the Promised Land—is the defining moment of the Old Testament. It is through the Exodus experience that the Jewish people come to know who they are and whose they are. Moses, of course, is God's point man for the job, going toe-to-toe with Pharaoh and demanding that he let God's people go. It is Moses who raises his arms for God to part the waters of the Red Sea so that the Jewish people could cross over from slavery to freedom. It is Moses to whom God gives the Ten Commandments to form His people into a nation."[1]

Let's backtrack a bit to understand why Jochebed found herself in such dire circumstances. Why were the Israelites enslaved in the first place?

Genesis 42 recounts a time when a severe famine spread across the land of Canaan. Under Joseph's leadership, the Israelites traveled to Egypt for food and subsequently settled there for hundreds of years. By the time we come to the book of Exodus, the Israelite population had increased to the point that Pharaoh felt threatened. He became consumed by irrational fears and delusional thoughts. Egyptian chronology is somewhat uncertain which Pharaoh was in office at this time, but the traditional view supports Thutmose 111 and Amunhotsep 11.[2]

The first chapter of Exodus outlines three strategies implemented by Pharaoh to suppress Israel. The first, a preemptive strike, singled out the rapidly expanding Hebrew minority as a perceived threat.

Exodus 1:8–14: "Then a new king, to whom Joseph meant nothing, came to power in Egypt. "Look," he said to his people, "the Israelites have become far too numerous for us. Come, we must deal shrewdly with them or they will become even more numerous and, if war breaks out, will join our enemies, fight against us and leave the country. But the more they were oppressed, the more they multiplied and spread; so the Egyptians came to dread the Israelites and worked them ruthlessly. They made their lives bitter with harsh labor in brick and mortar and with all kinds of work in the fields; in all their harsh labor the Egyptians worked them ruthlessly."

The Hebrew people, enslaved for 400 years, suffered cruel oppression and abuse under Egyptian rule. Pharaoh used slave labor to build two supply cities: Ramses and Pithom. The Israelites built channels for rivers, walls, ramparts, and the pyramids. However, Pharaoh's plan to weaken them and keep them from multiplying was unsuccessful.[3]

Incensed, Pharaoh instituted a second strategy: infanticide. As a deranged leader sought to destroy a people group, God used a powerful cross-cultural and intergenerational alliance of women to thwart him at every turn. Shiphrah and Puah carried the baton first. They became a part of Pharaoh's plan, entering our story in Exodus 1:15: "The king of Egypt said to the Hebrew midwives, whose names were Shiphrah and Puah, "When you are helping the Hebrew women during childbirth on the delivery stool, if you see that the baby is a boy, kill him; but if it is a girl, let her live." The midwives, however, feared God and did not do what the king of Egypt had told them to do; they let the boys live."

Pharaoh issued a royal decree to kill all male babies at birth as a program to control the population. Midwives, charged with the responsibility of bringing children into the world, dared to defy a king. The nationality of Shiphrah and Puah is ambiguous. Although we cannot be certain if they were Egyptian or Hebrew, the Jewish historian, Josephus, asserts they were Egyptian supervisors of 500-plus midwives.

"Hebrew midwives" can read, "midwives to the Hebrews," and as Egyptians, they would carry out Pharaoh's order. They were called in to oversee Hebrew births and commanded to carry out the unthinkable. Shiphrah means "to procreate" and Puah means "bearing of children." Their very vocation was to preserve and protect life. Whether they were

Hebrew or Egyptian, they were women who risked being punished by a wicked monarch capable of such an evil act. These midwives rebelled against Pharaoh by keeping the babies alive. Disobeying the direct order of a Pharaoh could result in the death and destruction of your entire family. Yet, these fearless women chose life. And in doing so, they played a crucial role in delivering a deliverer.

Can we just pause for a moment and sit with the gravity of their choice? What would propel these women past the possibility of death to stand up for justice?

Verse 17 tells us why: "They feared God."

The Hebrew word used here is "yare'", meaning to fear, honor, or be in awe. At first glance, it seems Shiphrah and Puah were mercilessly caught in the jaws of a culture in crisis. They found themselves in the center of a horrific moral dilemma. We aren't privy to the conversations they had behind closed doors. They certainly hadn't asked to be placed in the national spotlight. Yet please know, dear friends, that they were not there by chance. They were divinely positioned for change because God trusted their character. Their choice had consequences: they faced intense scrutiny for their actions.

V 18–19: "Why have you done this? Why have you let the boys live?" The midwives answered the Pharaoh, "Hebrew women are not like Egyptian women; they are vigorous and give birth before the midwives arrive."

Called before the king, they mustered the nerve to resist the will of Egypt's most powerful, sovereign ruler. Although they responded with a half-truth, it's important to note that their motivation for lying was to preserve life. They chose to stand up for the cause of protecting the Hebrew babies at the peril of their own lives. In doing so, they became a conduit for God's providence, His means of delivering the Hebrews.

Employed by Pharaoh and subject to his rage, they were commanded to remain instruments of barbarity. Yet, in striking contrast to the national practice of abortion and infanticide, their actions constitute the first act of civil disobedience—non-violent resistance—for the sake of justice. Given a heart-wrenching choice, they followed God. And God blessed them for their obedience.

V 20–21, "So God was kind to the midwives and the people increased and became even more numerous. And because the midwives feared God, he gave them families of their own."

These women lived ordinary lives but dared to do extraordinary things. They were fearless because they feared God. They simply did the right thing at the right time, and in doing so, they thwarted the enemy's plan. God is no respecter of persons. Whether they were Hebrew or Egyptian, God blessed them for their obedience and faith in Him. They used the one resource they had to protect life: their vocation. These two, seemingly powerless women stood up to outwit and outsmart a king. They knew a critical secret that shines hope into our struggles. Pharaoh was not in control; God was in control. The larger picture was to get Moses to his place of leadership. Did they recognize they were playing a vital part in God's divine plan to deliver a deliver? We'll never know. But we do know they stood up to defend the cause of those who could not defend themselves.

Perhaps you feel paralyzed by a decision you're facing, agonizing over your next move. If you're questioning why God has you in a particular position, take your cues from these heroic women. Courage stares into the face of uncertainty and does the next, right thing. We can stand up for justice at all costs when we fear God more than man. When the world contradicts the Word, the Word has the final say. **Our ordinary, everyday moments can become platforms for the miraculous when we choose obedience.**

Find Your Fearless

FEARLESS TAKEAWAY

Our ordinary, everyday moments can become platforms for the miraculous when we choose obedience.

FEARLESS NEXT STEPS

1. When we face confusing circumstances and tough decisions, we can wonder if we're up to the challenge. Describe an area of your life that is currently clouded by doubt.

2. 2 John 1:6 shows us what obedience looks like: "And this is love: that we walk in obedience to his commands. As you have heard from the beginning, his command is that you walk in love." Where is God asking you for greater obedience to Him?

3. Shiphrah and Puah used the one means they had to affect change in their culture: their vocation. What resources has God entrusted to you? Resist the temptation to dismiss what may seem ordinary. As you choose obedience, how can God use these resources for His purposes in your life and the lives of others?

FEARLESS DECLARATION

I will not allow doubt to cloud my decisions. I will be fearless because I fear God. I trust that my obedience will be the platform for the miraculous. I know God's Word has the final say.

FEARLESS PRAYER

My prayer in my words…

Her Choice—Stand Out

JOCHEBED

If the enemy is anything, he's persistent. He never stops at the first attempt to derail our destiny. Undeterred by Shiphrah and Puah's life-saving actions, Pharaoh's hostility intensified. As his first and second strategies failed, he implemented a third and final policy to defeat the Hebrew people.

In Exodus 1:22, the enemy's plan expanded from a concealed and concentrated effort to a national executive order. Pharaoh pivoted from the narrow, more controllable dictate given to the midwives to a broad mandate required of *all* his people.

"Then Pharaoh gave this order to all his people: "Every boy that is born you must throw into the Nile, but let every girl live."

Pharaoh's broadened attack incited neighbor against neighbor. Existing side by side in Goshen, the Israelites became integrated with the Egyptians over time. At this point in history, they co-existed together for 400 years in a culture that placed premium value on a woman's ability to bear a child. With one sentence, the joy of motherhood was stolen from every Hebrew woman.

Yet as Pharaoh attempted to take the most sacred of gifts, the opportunity to bring life, every attack was met with God's intervention. Let's pick up our story again in Exodus 2:1: "Now a man of the tribe of Levi married a Levite woman, and she became pregnant."

Pregnant. Let the plans begin.

Insert adorable baby shower invitations and ideas for a creative gender reveal party. Call that photographer that took that pregnancy photo shoot you loved. Post sonogram pics across your social media channels. Choose paint colors for the nursery and presents for your registry. Blissful moments savored by an excited, expectant mom.

But not for Jochebed.

She treasured the months leading up to the birth of her first child, a girl she named Miriam. She laughed at her expanding belly and marveled at every kick. But that was then. That was before the world started crumbling around her and her people. Now, not a day passed without grieving for one of her friends, crushed by the realization that they were pregnant. She watched their marriages splinter under the strain of the loss of intimacy. Secretly, she wondered if hers might be next. It had been years since she had carried Miriam. But she knew the signs immediately.

As the royal edict came down, Jochebed, a woman in slavery under a repressive dictator, found herself pregnant. The facts write the account of a woman with no recourse…no rights. But Scripture tells us a very different story.

Jochebed was a daughter of Levi, married to Amram, a Levite member of the priestly community. Jochebed means "Jehovah is her glory." This outwardly ordinary woman is the first person in Scripture to have a name compounded with "Jah" or "Jehovah,"—the name of God.[4]

Her name alone indicates she stood out from the crowd. Yet, all her knowledge of God was about to be tested like never before. Girls don't miss this. We can know who God is, but until we're asked to put that knowledge into action, we won't know the depth of our faith. **Faith is birthed in secret places when we choose trust over terror.**

She waited for nine months, without access to a sonogram. She had no way of knowing if the baby she was carrying was a boy or a girl until the instant she gave birth. How did she endure the waves of anxiety that must have washed over her in vulnerable moments? How did she handle the panic that threatened to set in when she delivered a son?

Scripture shares the weapon she wielded against fear. She was an ordinary woman giving birth in anything but ordinary conditions. And he was no ordinary child.

Exodus 2:2: "She gave birth to a son. When she saw that he was no ordinary child, she hid him for three months." In Acts 7, we read that she cared for him in her family home while he was still able to be kept relatively quiet. She nursed him in secret until she could hide him no longer. But Hebrews 11:23 provides another critical piece of information.

"By faith Moses' parents hid him for three months after he was born, because they saw he was no ordinary child, and they were not afraid of the king's edict."

In an unfathomable situation, she saw the fingerprints of an extraordinary God. She had heard the stories of the women who suffocated their own children before they allowed the Egyptians to take them. In a culture where confusion was screaming, Jochebed perceived the still small voice of Jehovah. She *saw* he was no ordinary child—she discerned—and looked for the open window of opportunity.

Not only was she present and perceptive, she was prepared for God's provision. Since she placed her trust in God, her spirit was equipped for the most daunting fight of her life. She practiced a personal relationship with Jehovah. *That* is why she was "not afraid of the king's edict." Because she stood on the foundation of faith, she stood out and seized her God-moment. This fearless mama crafted a clever design to preserve the life of her baby boy. Her courageous next steps impacted the destiny of a nation.

Exodus 2:3–4: "But when she could hide him no longer, she got a papyrus basket for him and coated it with tar and pitch. Then she placed the child in it and put it among the reeds along the bank of the Nile. His sister stood at a distance to see what would happen to him."

Jochebed's bold choice required her to go against every maternal instinct to place her baby in the Nile River. Not only did she risk her life and the lives of her family by violating Pharaoh's order, she endangered her baby by surrendering him to the Nile.

Let's stop for a second. Our thoughts might be tumbling, possibly landing on the premise that she had no choice. But, girls, we always have a choice. When we crumble under circumstances, we let the world have what is most precious to us. If our hope is not firmly set on God, our hearts will settle for less than His best.

She could've let Egypt take him or do the unspeakable and take matters into her own hands. Instead, she became an instrument of preservation and deliverance at her own peril. Instead of caving to the world's demands, she crafted a cradle to save hope. Think about the irony of her decision:

King's order = all babies thrown into Nile River.

Jochebed's plan = place baby into the Nile River.

But let's be clear. She didn't sacrifice him to the Nile; she surrendered him to Jehovah. Because she placed her hope in God, the enemy's plot for destruction became God's tool for preservation.

Her homemade cradle might be better described as a "mini-ark." The Hebrew box, or "chest" was made from finger-thick, bamboo-like pieces of papyrus stretching 10–15 feet tall. She reached for the same plant used by Egyptians to build light and swift boats. This tiny watercraft resembled a much larger vessel constructed by Noah as God's intended tool of preservation during a world-wide flood. And Jochebed's faith mirrors the faith of a young girl she would never meet. Mary followed in Jochebed's fearless footsteps when she gave birth to Jesus, God's means of preservation for all mankind. On a tiny stretch of a riverbank in Egypt, and in an insignificant cave in Bethlehem, the voice of hope rose above the noise of fear.

We're tempted to place our hope in so many things. People. Bank accounts. Promotions. A different spouse. A healthier body. But if we tether our trust to anything but God, we will find ourselves sorely disappointed. Fearless faith relies on God to make a way. No matter how insurmountable the odds seem against us, God can preserve our hope. When the future seemed grave, Jochebed made a critical choice that still speaks to us today.

She crouched in the weeds and held her breath. But that's not the whole story. Her desperation gave way to dependence on God, and her faith collided with destiny. She had carefully paid attention to the time and place Pharaoh's daughter typically bathed. As Miriam stood at a distance, the baton was passed once again.

Find Your Fearless

FEARLESS TAKEAWAY

Faith is birthed in secret places when we choose trust over terror.

FEARLESS NEXT STEPS

1. It's not until we're asked to put our knowledge of God into action that we test the depth of our faith. In what way is God asking you to stand out from the crowd and express faith through action?

2. Romans 5:2–5 states: "We boast in the hope of the glory of God. Not only so, but we also glory in our sufferings, because we know that suffering produces perseverance; perseverance, character; and character, hope. And hope does not put us to shame, because God's love has been poured out into our hearts through the Holy Spirit, who has been given to us." Another translation puts it this way: "Hope does not disappoint." Identify any area of your life where you sense the voice of hope being drowned out by your circumstances. How might the awareness that God is pouring His love over you change your beliefs about Him and His purposes?

3. What are the secret places where you tend to place your hope in a source other than God? Practice surrender and tether those tender places to God.

FEARLESS DECLARATION

I acknowledge that I always have a choice. I will make choices inspired by faith instead of fear. I believe that God is making a way as I depend on His faithfulness.

FEARLESS PRAYER

My prayer in my words…

Her Catalyst for Change—Stand Strong

A TALE OF TWO DAUGHTERS

It was just another ordinary day. Their spirited conversation stood in stark contrast to the hushed laments mere yards away. Pharaoh's daughter and her attendants chatted casually about how the weather seemed more muggy than normal and how awful the humidity was for their hair. They caught up on budding relationships and adjusted their sandals to manage the thick soil. You know…the usual stuff. Their feet had walked these steps on many occasions, their usual path for their usual time to bathe.

But today, this ordinary moment turned into an unexpected encounter, divinely orchestrated by God.

We'll pick up our story in Exodus 2:5–6: "Then Pharaoh's daughter went down to the Nile to bathe, and her attendants were walking along the riverbank. She saw the basket among the reeds and sent her female slave to get it. She opened it and saw the baby. He was crying, and she felt sorry for him. "This is one of the Hebrew babies," she said."

And in that split second, the baton was passed. Darby's concordance puts it this way: "Providence responds to faith and provides an answer."[5] The moment she drew him out of the water, she became an enemy of the state. Historical records leave it unclear as to the identity of Pharaoh's daughter. Yet, since we are certain it is the 18th dynasty, she is either Thermutis or Hatshepsut.[6]

What would motivate her to take such drastic action with monumental consequences? Perhaps it was a spur of the moment decision. Or, it's possible she had contemplated this very scenario. We can't know for certain, but most historical and theological writings consistently support several claims.

First, it's highly plausible that Pharaoh had only a daughter and no sons. If that was the case, she was potentially influenced by a political move to acquire an heir. By taking the baby left helplessly in the water, she would gain an adopted heir who could protect her father's dynasty and give her a legitimate right to rule. The probability of this scenario is offset slightly by the tremendous risk she took by disregarding the order of the king...who just happened to be her father.

Even though she was old enough to reside in her own royal living quarters, it's unlikely she could hide this event from Pharaoh. She pushed past the rage she would inevitably encounter, pointing us to another possible purpose in her daring rescue. She may have reached for him simply out of compassion and desire for social justice. Scripture says, "She felt sorry for him." She stood up against her father's order, strategically placing herself between the crying child and certain death. She stood out from Egyptian culture and enabled all the women carrying the baton to stand strong.

Whether her actions were self-serving to secure an heir or selfless to save a child, God used her to become a catalyst for change. It didn't matter that she was Egyptian, and this helpless baby was Hebrew. Refusing to be defined by racial bigotry or religious discrimination, she took a bold step that altered the course of history.

But this is a tale of not one, but two daughters, who fearlessly put themselves in harm's way. Let's continue our story in Exodus 2:7—10.

Remember Jochebed's first child, Miriam? She made the journey with her mother to the water's edge and waited for her turn to carry the baton. Was her little heart beating out of her chest? Did she wonder if there was a chance this plan wouldn't work? I imagine she kept low to the ground, cautiously observant, moving on her mom's cue. Miriam believed against all odds that the words her mother uttered in faith were true: *God will provide.*

And while water still dripped off the edge of the basket, Miriam spoke up for her brother. "Shall I get one of the Hebrew women to nurse the baby for you?"

"Yes, go," she answered. And the girl went and got the baby's mother. Pharaoh's daughter said to her, "Take this baby and nurse him for me, and I will pay you." So the woman took the baby and nursed him. When the child grew older, she took him to Pharaoh's daughter, and he became her son. She named him Moses, saying, "I drew him out of the water."

Not only did God provide Pharaoh's daughter as a means of rescue, he made a way for Jochebed to enjoy him without fear. She became an integral part of his upbringing, even rewarded financially to nurse him. She was paid a wage to care for him for a minimum of three years, and as many as seven. Jochebed's choices preserved God's destiny and protected the call on his life. But she had to hand him over to Egypt. Pharaoh's daughter loved him and raised him as her own.

Acts 7:21—22 tell us that Moses was saturated in the culture of Egypt. "Pharaoh's daughter took him and brought him up as her own son. Moses was educated in all the wisdom of the Egyptians and was powerful in speech and action." She served as the chief influence in his life, offering him the highest level of training and 40 years of royal protection.

Jochebed gave him the roots of a godly foundation necessary for all God would eventually ask of him. She birthed Moses, the greatest national leader of all time and Aaron, the first High Priest. And the little girl, Miriam, served by Moses' side as a gifted prophetess, poet and musician. He had both a birth and an adoptive mother who loved him deeply—caught in the crosshairs of a culture in crisis. God's plan called for both to act fearlessly to save him from a cruel death and preserve him for a unique life.

Each woman ran their leg of the baton race for the greater good. The midwives stood strong under great duress. Miriam stood strong under dangerous conditions. Jochebed stood strong when the time came to give him back. And Pharaoh's daughter stood strong against the dictates of her own father.

Their legacy teaches us a powerful truth: ordinary moments become extraordinary when our obedience intersects with God's provision. We learn how to flex our faith muscles by saying yes to God in small decisions. Then, when we're faced with a giant "ask," we're ready because we've consistently developed trust. Knowing God's character helps us to trust Him in those "take-a-deep-breath-how-is-this-thing-going-to-work-out" times in our lives.

God's plan is greater than the enemy's plan. **God does His best work when we let go and get out of the way.** Moses' parents believed he was destined for God's purpose and surrendered him to the God they trusted to fulfill it. And fulfill it, He did.

Hebrews 11:24—28 shares a glimpse into Moses' future: "By faith Moses, when he had grown up, refused to be known as the son of Pharaoh's daughter. He chose to be mistreated along with the people of God rather than to enjoy the fleeting pleasures of sin. He regarded disgrace for the sake of Christ as of greater value than the treasures of Egypt, because he was looking ahead to his reward. By faith he left Egypt, not fearing the king's anger; he persevered because he saw him who is invisible. By faith he kept the Passover and the application of blood, so that the destroyer of the firstborn would not touch the firstborn of Israel."

He gave it all up: the wealth, the power, and the position. After Pharaoh's daughter raised him, he followed his God-given destiny and refused to be known as her son. Both Jochebed and Moses' adoptive mother experienced heartbreak to keep hope alive at all cost. A key phrase in the above passage might shed light on his decision: "By faith he left Egypt, not fearing the king's anger; he persevered because he saw him who is invisible."

If those words sound familiar, they should. They're the very words penned about Moses' parents when they hid their son. Years later, that child hid in the cleft of a rock while God's glory passed by. God spoke through him and used him mightily. The faith instilled in him as a child enabled him to conquer his own fears and deliver millions of people out of slavery and into the Promised Land. He learned by example that faith can overcome any obstacle and break through any barrier. All because a handful of ordinary women dared to do extraordinary things.

Find Your Fearless

FEARLESS TAKEAWAY

God does His best work when we let go and get out of the way.

FEARLESS NEXT STEPS

1. Pharaoh's daughter refused to be defined by racial bigotry or religious discrimination. Cultural issues gave her every reason to be stingy with her level of involvement, yet she let go of stigma and became a catalyst for change. How does her example challenge you to offer compassion generously within your culture?

2. 2 Corinthians 4:17–18 encourages our fragile hearts when surrender involves an agonizing choice: "For our light and momentary troubles are achieving for us an eternal glory that far outweighs them all. So we fix our eyes not on what is seen, but on what is unseen, since what is seen is temporary, but what is unseen is eternal." Jochebed gave up Moses, and Moses gave up Egypt, "because he was looking ahead to his reward." They surrendered the temporal to secure the eternal. Where do you need to release your grip on life so God's plans can be realized?

3. Each woman fearlessly ran their leg of the race and stood strong in the face of extreme pressure. What does your leg of the race look like right now? In what way do you need the Holy Spirit to empower you to stand strong? He invites us to ask and stirs us to act.

FEARLESS DECLARATION

I will be known for my compassion and heart for others. I will flex my faith muscles by saying yes to God in my everyday decisions, so I'm prepared for the big asks. I will surrender even the people and things most precious to me so God can do His best work.

FEARLESS PRAYER

My prayer in my words…

Their Calling and Ours

Through our study of the women who delivered a deliverer, we've seen that God can preserve our hope. The story of these women we've come to know and admire involves delicate problems still pressing us today. We can find our fearless as we explore the ways their calling influences ours.

Each woman recognized the short window of opportunity afforded to them to stand up against the challenges of her culture. They understood the risk but stepped out in faith and obedience to do the right thing at the right time. They seized their moment through critical choices that served as a catalyst for change. Their willingness to carry the baton influenced a nation and changed the course of history.

Let's consider some of the cultural issues we have in common with these remarkable women. Too often, we let these challenges build barriers that keep us from fearless living. Instead, let's use them to build bridges that carry us to our greatest impact.

MAKE A DENT

Looking at a landscape marred by racial tension and inequities in the global economy can paralyze us. It's natural to feel frustrated or even helpless in the face of uncertainty. But we must move past that place and embrace ways we can make a dent. In an age of widespread terrorism, fear can easily dispel faith. No one understood this more than Jochebed.

As a Hebrew woman in Egyptian culture, she was marginalized and victimized. She fell prey to persecution at the hands of a dictator who trampled the value of women. She didn't hold the power, but she did hold on to faith. Faith frames a situation through the truth of the Word instead of the narrative of the world. Whether we're fighting for our marriage, finding ways to eradicate poverty, or freeing victims of injustice, our foundation is faith. When we know God's voice, we develop the God-confidence we need to act.

Let's learn to recognize two traps often set by fear that keep us from responding to God's call.

WE OVERTHINK AND UNDER-ACT

Perhaps you've heard the phrase, "analysis paralysis." It is both wise and prudent to research and know the facts in a given situation. However, if we allow ourselves to become overwhelmed, we'll get stuck and never stand up. Fear tells us to walk away or choose passivity when we're not sure what to do next. It's critical that we train our ear to hear the voice of the Holy Spirit through prayer and the Word. He will guide us when we're reacting too slowly due to anxiety. He will help us distinguish whether the sense to pause is driven by divine prompting or deadly paralysis.

We underthink and over-act.

In contrast, we can rush ahead of God's timing when we don't first seek His heart in a situation. Fear is tricky. Not only can it cause us to delay, it can urge us to act impulsively and overstep our boundaries. If we are going to be fearless women of God, we must know His voice, sense His timing, and obey His Word. Each woman in our story demonstrates the importance of knowing when we need to wait or take our hands off something and let God work. We don't always know the story God is writing, which is why we have to let Him hold the pen. We can release our children, health, finances, and any other area we hold dear, when we trust our heavenly Father. As we allow Him to dictate our choices, we'll operate in godly discernment.

These three questions will help us to best follow God's call on our lives, especially in confusing circumstances. Answering honestly before we act will help ensure we don't lag behind His will or rush ahead of it.

Have I spent time waiting on God and reading His Word to know when He's guiding me to act?

Is fear holding me back from obeying God's voice?

Is this the open door designed by God or am I pushing it open?

MAKE A DECISION

Once we've asked ourselves those questions, we can take our next steps. Even baby steps are steps. We don't all wear the same shoe size, so we won't all leave the same footprint. My size 9 isn't your size 7½. But every imprint matters.

Understand, beautiful friend, that each role is important. We minimize someone else's contribution—or our own—when we become blinded by comparison. This is one way we miss the opportunity to seize God-moments. When we think we have to be seen, we've lost sight of the story God is writing. Girls, let's be okay with playing a supporting role instead of clamoring for the limelight. Let's decide to run *our* leg of the race, whatever it may be.

Your greatest opportunity to shape a culture is to do exactly what God has called you to do. Some of us will travel the globe until our passport can't hold another stamp to take a stand for justice. Others of us will travel the stairs in our homes until the carpet is threadbare to take care of our children. You are teachers and entrepreneurs and nurturers and friends. You are fearless mamas and brave sisters.

What makes us strong is not *what* we do, but *whether* we do what God has uniquely called us to do. Let's be willing to play a small part for the greater good. Don't spend one more second worrying about what someone else is doing. You're not them. Don't let comparison keep you from operating in the gifts God has deposited in *you*. Make the decision to obey God at all costs. When obedience is our criteria, we all win.

MAKE A DIFFERENCE

Can't you just hear Jochebed cheering you on? She's clapping wildly on the sidelines as you run your leg of the race. "Hold on tight to that baton, girl! Keep going! You're doing awesome!" Goodness, how we wonder at times if we're running in vain. Girls, we hear her speaking hope into our fragile hearts because she's been there, too.

She didn't need to be noticed to know she was making an eternal difference. She was willing to raise Moses in his formative years without anyone knowing she was his mother. She made the decision to fulfill her calling by helping Moses fulfill his. When we are kingdom minded, we aren't tempted to be earthly motivated.

Like the women we've studied, keep your eyes peeled for the miracle in the mundane. No matter what life throws at you, God can preserve your hope. Perhaps when you least expect it, He will breathe on that ordinary moment and leave you astounded.

> *That moment of leaning in to listen to a broken-hearted friend.*
> *That moment of leaving no stone unturned until the job is done right.*
> *That moment of loving your children unconditionally.*
> *That moment of letting your husband know you'd do it all again.*
> *That moment of leveraging your position to influence culture.*

Your moment looks different than mine. And your calling looks different than mine. We're called to be evangelists. And prayer warriors. And gap-fillers. And behind-the-scenes servants. And bold-hearted leaders. Faith compels us to step out in obedience. And when we do, we'll find our calling.

Any woman who chooses obedience is a rock star in God's book. And Jochebed isn't the only one whooping and hollering as you kick fear to the curb. I'm running alongside you, determined to do this together. Heavens, you inspire me. Keep carrying your baton with confidence and grace.

Find Your Fearless

FEARLESS TAKEAWAY

Your greatest opportunity to shape a culture is to do exactly what God has called you to do.

FEARLESS NEXT STEPS

1. Fear often sets two traps that keep us from responding to God's call: we overthink and under-act or we underthink and over-act. Which more easily trips you up and how can you make more faith-based decisions?

2. Romans 12:4–6 states, "For just as each of us has one body with many members, and these members do not all have the same function, so in Christ we, though many, form one body, and each member belongs to all the others. We have different gifts, according to the grace given to each of us." Comparison chokes out our calling. What baby step can you take right now toward your calling? Who inspires you and who can you inspire to keep running?

3. Reflect on a current situation where confusion is threatening your ability to make a clear decision. Answer the questions posed in our study honestly.

    Have I spent time waiting on God and reading His Word to know when He's guiding me to act?

    Is fear holding me back from obeying God's voice?

    Is this the open door designed by God or am I pushing it open?

FEARLESS DECLARATION

I will stop allowing my choices to be influenced by fear. Through the help of the Holy Spirit, I will make a dent, make a decision, and make a difference. I will stop listening to the voice of comparison and pursue God's calling on my life. I will offer gratitude for those who inspire me and pray that my life inspires others.

FEARLESS PRAYER

My prayer in my words...

Rahab

Her Story & Our Starting Place

> **Our past doesn't have to paralyze our future.**

JOSHUA 2

Before you begin your study, view the companion video resource here:

www.angeladonadio.com

I have also included the video message and our key Scripture passage below.

Welcome back, girlfriends! This week we're leaving Egypt and journeying over 200 miles into the Promised Land! Moses led God's people for 40 years through the wilderness, but Joshua took them across the Jordan River to possess the land given to them by God. First, they had to conquer Jericho—a critical, heavily fortified city and the key to all the land west of the Jordan.

They sent spies ahead to see what they faced. These men met a woman carrying a painful past and an uncertain future. They discovered the prostitute, Rahab, the unlikeliest of heroes with uncommon faith. She was stuck—in a sinful lifestyle, and in a wicked place, both set for destruction. Rahab dreamt of a different life; one where her worth was defined by what God said about her, not by the world. She put herself in grave danger to help the Israelites. Jericho is the place that God intersected her story with grace.

 Live From Jericho

Welcome to Jericho, one of the oldest cities in the world! It sits in the wide plain of the Jordan Valley, at the foot of the Judaean mountains. Jesus passed through this place, when he healed Bartimaeus of blindness and met Zacchaeus. But thousands of years earlier, an ordinary woman named Rahab lived within Jericho's walls. Imagine behind me a mound 9 acres wide, surrounded by a stone wall 12—15 feet high. Then on top of that, a mudbrick wall 6 feet thick and nearly 26 feet high. This was the impossible task the Israelites faced. In a city that was tightly closed up, God found a woman with an open heart. If it wasn't for the fearless faith of a prostitute named Rahab, we might not be reading this story today.

Let's look at Joshua Chapter 2.

Then Joshua son of Nun secretly sent two spies from Shittim. "Go, look over the land," he said, "especially Jericho." So they went and entered the house of a prostitute named Rahab and stayed there.

The king of Jericho was told, "Look, some of the Israelites have come here tonight to spy out the land." So the king of Jericho sent this message to Rahab: "Bring out the men who came to you and entered your house, because they have come to spy out the whole land."

But the woman had taken the two men and hidden them. She said, "Yes, the men came to me, but I did not know where they had come from. At dusk, when it was time to close the city gate, they left. I don't know which way they went. Go after them quickly. You may catch up with them." (But she had taken them up to the roof and hidden them under the stalks of flax she had laid out on the roof.) So the men set out in pursuit of the spies on the road that leads to the fords of the Jordan, and as soon as the pursuers had gone out, the gate was shut.

Before the spies lay down for the night, she went up on the roof and said to them, "I know that the Lord has given you this land and that a great fear of you has fallen on us, so that all who live in this country are melting in fear because of you. We have heard how the Lord dried up the water of the Red Sea[a] for you when you came out of Egypt, and what you did to Sihon and Og, the two kings of the Amorites east of the Jordan, whom you completely destroyed. When we heard of it, our hearts melted in fear and everyone's courage failed because of you, for the Lord your God is God in heaven above and on the earth below. Now then, please swear to me by the Lord that you will show kindness to my family, because I have shown kindness to you. Give me a sure sign that you will spare the lives of my father and mother, my brothers and sisters, and all who belong to them—and that you will save us from death."

"Our lives for your lives!" the men assured her. "If you don't tell what we are doing, we will treat you kindly and faithfully when the Lord gives us the land."

So she let them down by a rope through the window, for the house she lived in was part of the city wall. She said to them, "Go to the hills so the pursuers will not find you. Hide yourselves there three days until they return, and then go on your way."

Now the men had said to her, "This oath you made us swear will not be binding on us unless, when we enter the land, you have tied this scarlet cord in the window through which you let us down, and unless you have brought your father and mother, your brothers and all your family into your house. If any of them go outside your house into the street, their blood will be on their own heads; we will not be responsible. As for those who are in the house with you, their blood will be on our head if a hand is laid on them. But if you tell what we are doing, we will be released from the oath you made us swear."

"Agreed," she replied. "Let it be as you say."

So she sent them away, and they departed. And she tied the scarlet cord in the window.

When they left, they went into the hills and stayed there three days, until the pursuers had searched all along the road and returned without finding them. Then the two men started back. They went down out of the hills, forded the river and came to Joshua son of Nun and told him everything that had happened to them. They said to Joshua, "The Lord has surely given the whole land into our hands; all the people are melting in fear because of us."

I'm so challenged by the courage of Rahab. It's much easier to just blend in with the crowd than to stand up for what is right. We'll read the rest of this story together and get to know a woman who stood out—and dared to do extraordinary things—because of her faith.

I sat mere feet from the only structure that remained when the walls of Jericho collapsed. As the brutal noonday sun beat across my face, one simple fact arrested my thoughts: a house built strategically against the town wall stood when the walls fell. Yet, even more incredulous, one woman, under the intense heat of pressure and her back against the wall, refused to bow to fear.

Rahab wanted out of this place.

She devised a plan, not out of selfishness, but out of authentic faith. The sign of her willingness and complete cooperation was a scarlet cord, hanging conspicuously in her window. No matter how strong the enemy looked on the outside, her faith remained intact on the inside.

Our past doesn't have to paralyze our future. You can get out from under anything that's trying to bury you. When you encounter Christ, you are freed from the identity put on you by the world. Rahab beautifully demonstrates how God intersects our story with grace.

\\|/

Our past
DOESN'T
HAVE TO
paralyze our
future.

Her Cause—Stand Up

Rahab brushed her long, chestnut-brown hair and pulled it taut at the nape of her neck. She tied it firmly with a crimson ribbon of fabric and felt her shoulders twinge from holding so much tension. Her hands dropped heavy into her lap as her frame exhaled deeply. She closed her eyes and allowed herself to imagine what it might be like to be somewhere else...any place where she mattered.

She couldn't remember the last time she wasn't tired. It was bad enough to be trapped inside a city where no one could move in or out. But she knew it was her own choices that entombed her most.

She pressed her hand against the door, built against the city wall.

"So close yet impossible," she thought with resignation. She longed for a fresh start and wondered if a conversation she overheard just days before might hold the answer.

"We must remain vigilant. We have enough supplies to last through a siege, even if it goes on for a couple of months. With what the Israelites have done to our neighbors, we can't risk them infiltrating our city. And after their escape through the Red Sea, who knows what could happen? The ban stays. No one goes in, no one goes out."

The tremor in the men's voices exposed their fear, but something inside of her leapt at the possibilities. Could this be her chance for a clean slate?

Who was this improbable heroine? Although some Jewish and Christian writers have tried to assert that Rahab was an innkeeper, the Hebrew "zunah" is translated prostitute. She was at the bottom of the social ladder and considered less than human. Yet God knew something about her that no one else recognized. Rahab, a Gentile, stood poised to receive both the Israelite people and their God.

Moses, the great deliverer, was dead. He led the people to the edge of the promised land but a new leader, Joshua, carried the charge to take them in. A military genius, he detained the people at Shittim, in the plains of Moab. They halted at the last camping place east of the Jordan, just three hours from the crossing place while Joshua sent two spies ahead to ascertain the task ahead.

They openly declared to the Edomites and Moabites living in the region that they were seeking a settlement in Canaan. The Kings of Sihon and Og refused to allow them safe passageway and were quickly defeated. As the knowledge of their conquest gained traction throughout the area, the King of Jericho prepared for a siege. This large, fortified city sat a mere eight miles from the Jordan River. As fear clenched its grip on Jericho, the King restricted any movement in or out of the city.

Joshua secretly sent two spies to investigate the land, especially Jericho, the most important Canaanite fortress city in the Jordan Valley. This stronghold was a critical conquest for the Israelites and a principal seat of idol worship. The people inside Jericho's walls engaged in vile, degrading behavior including child sacrifice to honor Ashtaroth, the goddess of the moon, and Ra, the Egyptian sun god.

As our story unfolds in Joshua 2:1, the stakes couldn't be higher for either side. "So they went and entered the house of a prostitute name Rahab and stayed there."

Let's just park right here for a moment and address the obvious. Why would the spies stop here? Three theories emerge:

They anonymously sought prostitution. Hmmm. Possible, but highly unlikely considering they represented Joshua on an urgent mission with spiritual ramifications.

They hunted for a place where they could visit without suspicion. Bearing in mind Rahab's profession, male visitors wouldn't raise any eyebrows.

Or perhaps they chose this site for its strategic advantages. Ideally located as part of the city wall, it provided a swift escape route.

It's here, in a wicked city under condemnation, that God marvelously interrupted Rahab's story with grace. At first glance, it seems like anything but an ideal circumstance to come to faith. But God isn't limited by walls—of any kind. She was part of a corrupt culture, but she leveraged a critical asset: she used what she overheard. News of the Israelites exploits spread like wildfire throughout the city. She believed it was too late for her city. But now, the God she heard about stood at her front door in the form of two spies.

Not only was she observant, she was prepared for this unexpected, divine encounter. With the pull of a thousand distractions and a terrified city against her, she was a determined woman on a mission. And her grit intersected God's grace.

Perceptive, intelligent, and well-informed, Rahab seized the moment presented to her and saw her opportunity to get out. She didn't want to be a part of this culture anymore. She knew that to stay meant certain death. She ached for a life without shame, without stigma, and without shackles. So with laser focus, she embraced the window given to her to become a follower of Yahweh by welcoming them into her home.

Look at her words in verses 8—11: "Before the spies lay down for the night, she went up on the roof and said to them, "I know that the Lord has given you this land and that a great fear of you has fallen on us, so that all who live in this country are melting in fear because of you. We have heard how the Lord dried up the water of the Red Sea for you when you came out of Egypt, and what you did to Sihon and Og, the two kings of the Amorites east of the Jordan, whom you completely destroyed. When we heard of it, our hearts melted in fear and everyone's courage failed because of you, for the Lord your God is God in heaven above and on the earth below."

Her cause wasn't just the promise of a new life; it was truth. It was her faith in God that enabled her to be fearless. She rose above inordinate pressure, putting herself and her family in grave danger to assist the spies. Her belief in God became the impetus for action. She could "see" Israel conquering Jericho. I love how the commentator Barnes describes it: "The same news that terrifies the leadership and people of Jericho inspires her to faith and conversion."[7]

Her faith was ready; all it needed was an opportunity. She remained calm and composed while she dared to brave the fury of the King and her people. Everyone heard about the miracles surrounding the Israelites. But only Rahab believed.

The proof is in the passage.

Verse 9: "I know the Lord has given you the land." = Her revelation that it is already done.

Verse 11: "The Lord your God is God in heaven above and on the earth below." = Her confession that she has already decided.

The book of James paints a powerful picture of faith in action. And he includes our girl, Rahab, in his description of what it looks like to operate in faith.

James 2: 14—26: "What good is it, my brothers and sisters, if someone claims to have faith but has no deeds? Can such faith save them? Suppose a brother or a sister is without clothes and daily food. If one of you says to them, "Go in peace; keep warm and well fed," but does nothing about their physical needs, what good is it? In the same way, faith by itself, if it is not accompanied by action, is dead.

But someone will say, "You have faith; I have deeds." Show me your faith without deeds, and I will show you my faith by my deeds. You believe that there is one God. Good! Even the demons believe that—and shudder.

You foolish person, do you want evidence that faith without deeds is useless? Was not our father Abraham considered righteous for what he did when he offered his son Isaac on the altar? You see that his faith and his actions were working together, and his faith was made complete by what he did. And the scripture was fulfilled that says, "Abraham believed God, and it was credited to him as righteousness," and he was called God's friend. You see that a person is considered righteous by what they do and not by faith alone.

In the same way, was not even Rahab the prostitute considered righteous for what she did when she gave lodging to the spies and sent them off in a different direction? As the body without the spirit is dead, so faith without deeds is dead."

Bottom line? **Faith acts. Fear makes excuses.** Rahab didn't just believe from a distance; she opened the front door. Because she was willing to stand up against impossible odds to do the right thing, she was considered righteous by God. She traded her bruised identity for a bold beginning. The world branded her by a painful past, but God believed in her potential.

Girls, faith sharpens our discernment and clarifies our vision. When society tries to define us by our past, God points us to our future. It's particularly difficult when our reputation has been tarnished by what others have done to us or by what we have done to ourselves. Shame shoves us back behind closed doors and mocks us for dreaming of a different life. Faith pulls us out of our hiding places and propels us into our calling. This kind of faith is based upon our belief in a loving, kind God who cares about us.

Trust me. Our story is just getting good. We have a lot more to learn from our fierce girl, Rahab. Not only did she welcome the spies, she lied for them, protected them, and left with them. Rahab knew she was meant for more; and so are you. If she could rise above her past, so can we. If she could crush her fear, so can we. If she could stand up against the depravity of her culture and dare to stand up for God, so can we.

\\\|//

Find Your Fearless

FEARLESS TAKEAWAY

Faith acts. Fear makes excuses.

FEARLESS NEXT STEPS

1. Rahab maintained laser focus to embrace the window of opportunity she was given. In what way might you need to remove distractions to see God-ordained moments more clearly?

2. James includes Rahab in his description of what it looks like to operate in faith. She didn't believe from a distance; she took up the cause of the Israelites and acted courageously on their behalf. With her as our example, chew on his words, "As the body without the spirit is dead, so faith without deeds is dead." Is there an area of your life God is compelling you to act?

3. Shame shoves us back behind closed doors and mocks us for dreaming of a different life. Faith pulls us out of our hiding places and propels us into our calling. Could a painful part of your past or present challenge be holding you back? If so, ask God to remove the sting of shame and resurrect those places with His grace.

FEARLESS DECLARATION

I will not allow shame to keep me from pursuing God's call on my life. I will allow God's grace to intersect my painful places with His grace. I will choose to stand up for what is right even when I'm the only one. I know I am meant for more.

FEARLESS PRAYER

My prayer in my words...

Her Choice—Stand Out

As Rahab took her first steps toward embracing her God-sized dreams, the plot thickened across town. Word travels fast in a shut-up city, and it didn't take long for the scoop about our out-of-town guests to make it to the king's palace.

Verse 2–7: "The king of Jericho was told, "Look, some of the Israelites have come here tonight to spy out the land." So the king of Jericho sent this message to Rahab: "Bring out the men who came to you and entered your house, because they have come to spy out the whole land." But the woman had taken the two men and hidden them. She said, "Yes, the men came to me, but I did not know where they had come from. At dusk, when it was time to close the city gate, they left. I don't know which way they went. Go after them quickly. You may catch up with them." (But she had taken them up to the roof and hidden them under the stalks of flax she had laid out on the roof.) So the men set out in pursuit of the spies on the road that leads to the fords of the Jordan, and as soon as the pursuers had gone out, the gate was shut."

Rahab was given a clear directive from the highest office in the land. With nerves of steel, she stared straight ahead and made a life-altering choice: she lied for the spies. She didn't have to think twice. Her decision, tantamount to treason, was firmly fastened to faith.

I did not know where they came from.
They left.
I don't know which way they went.
Go after them quickly.

With a few strategic statements, Rahab began to etch a name for herself in God's book of heroines. She hadn't applied for this job position, and she didn't earn it. God chose her for this assignment and used her assertiveness. She wasn't intimidated by what stood in front of her or shackled by what lay in her past. None of that mattered. She stood out by acting on simple faith that was given space to breathe.

She played dumb and boldly lied to the messengers of the king. However, just like the midwives in Egypt, her choice was motivated by selflessness and rooted in genuine trust. Scripture doesn't condemn her for telling a falsehood; it commends her for her faith. She had a clear understanding of who the spies were and knew their plan was to overthrow the city. Not only did she welcome them and lie for them, she protected them at the risk of her own life. She wasn't foolish; she was fearless.

As soon as she heard the clanging of the closing gate, she rushed to the roof. Pulling back thick stalks of flax, more than three feet in height, she revealed the hidden spies. Previously, we read the first words that tumbled from her lips, as she confidently declared Jehovah as the One true God. And in the conversation that followed, she outlined a proposal that guaranteed her protection in return for theirs.

Verse 12: "Now then, please swear to me by the Lord that you will show kindness to my family, because I have shown kindness to you. Give me a sure sign that you will spare the lives of my father and mother, my brothers and sisters, and all who belong to them—and that you will save us from death."

"Our lives for your lives!" the men assured her. "If you don't tell what we are doing, we will treat you kindly and faithfully when the Lord gives us the land."

So she let them down by a rope through the window, for the house she lived in was part of the city wall. She said to them, "Go to the hills so the pursuers will not find you. Hide yourselves there three days until they return, and then go on your way."

Now the men had said to her, "This oath you made us swear will not be binding on us unless, when we enter the land, you have tied this scarlet cord in the window through which you let us down, and unless you have brought your father and mother, your brothers and all your family into your house. If any of them go outside your house into the street, their blood will be on their own heads; we will not be responsible.

As for those who are in the house with you, their blood will be on our head if a hand is laid on them. But if you tell what we are doing, we will be released from the oath you made us swear."

"Agreed," she replied. "Let it be as you say."

So she sent them away, and they departed. And she tied the scarlet cord in the window."

Oh, to have been a fly on the wall—er, the roof. Can't you just hear the epic musical score accompanying this dramatic scene? As the tension mounted, Rahab demanded an oath and described a plan. Before another word could be spoken, she needed to know one thing: swear to me you'll spare me. Promise—before God—that you'll remember me and my family with kindness.

Kindness. What an interesting choice of words. "Show kindness to my family, because I have shown kindness to you." And the spies responded in turn: Don't tell anyone, and we'll treat you kindly and faithfully.

Let's linger on this thought for a hot minute. The Hebrew word for kindness, "hesed," means loyalty, or to come alongside someone to pick them up. Found in several places throughout Scripture, one of the most poignant examples is in 2 Samuel 9. King Saul, the ruler in Israel at the time, was killed in battle alongside his son, Jonathan. His death closed a bitter chapter in which jealousy of David drove him mad and robbed him of God's anointing. With his death, David, God's appointed heir, ascended the throne. Yet, despite all Saul did to make David's life utterly miserable, David looked for an opportunity to bless his descendants on account of his friendship with Jonathan.

Seeking out one of Saul's servants, Ziba, David asked, "Is there no one still alive from the house of Saul to whom I can show God's kindness?" Ziba answered the king, "There is still a son of Jonathan; he is lame in both feet."

When most wouldn't bat an eye walking away, David wouldn't rest until he found Mephibosheth.

"Don't be afraid," David said to him, "for I will surely show you kindness for the sake of your father Jonathan. I will restore to you all the land that belonged to your grandfather Saul, and you will always eat at my table."

Kindness is the vehicle that transports favor. When someone has little or nothing to offer, kindness steps in and bridges the gap. It goes above and beyond expectations and carves out a path for the miraculous to follow.

Titus 3 recounts the greatest act of kindness: "At one time we too were foolish, disobedient, deceived and enslaved by all kinds of passions and pleasures. We lived in malice and envy, being hated and hating one another. But when the kindness and love of God our Savior appeared, he saved us, not because of righteous things we had done, but because of his mercy. He saved us through the washing of rebirth and renewal by the Holy Spirit, whom he poured out on us generously through Jesus Christ our Savior, so that, having been justified by his grace, we might become heirs having the hope of eternal life."

The kindness and love of God our Savior appeared in the form of Jesus Christ. He stepped in to save us when we had nothing to offer. And just like Rahab, we didn't earn it. His death on the cross bridged the gap that we could never fix on our own. His resurrection meant we, like Mephibosheth, would always have a seat at His table. It's the kindness and love of God that rescued Rahab, found Mephibosheth, and saves us.

Yet our rescue, just like Rahab's, is conditional upon one thing: accepting Jesus as our Savior. Her protection was contingent on her obedience. Their plan to spare her involved three requirements:

Tie a scarlet rope in your window.
Make sure you and your family are inside the house.
Don't breathe a word of what we're doing.

With their lives literally hanging by a thread, a thin, scarlet cord became the designated sign of her commitment and cooperation.

In "The Scarlet Cord of Redemption," Carter Corbrey describes it this way:

> A slim scarlet cord dangling in a window might not trigger thoughts of deliverance. That is, unless you were Rahab, a Gentile woman living in a home built into the wall of the ancient city of Jericho over three thousand years ago. Rahab's scarlet cord was a sign to the approaching Hebrew armies to spare her family because she did not put her faith in walls, but in the God of Israel. When she encountered two Hebrew spies who had come to scout the city, she chose to be on the winning side.

That scarlet cord represented redemption for a handful of Gentiles. Yet it also symbolized a greater deliverance. Threaded throughout the Old Testament is a "scarlet cord" of Scripture, foretelling redemption through Jesus, the Jewish Messiah. He came to hang on Calvary, even as that scarlet cord hung from the window. Through Him alone, Jews and Gentiles can find redemption from sin.[8]

It wasn't enough for Rahab to make a promise; she had to put her faith on display for all to see. She fearlessly followed their directions to a T. Girls, it's not enough for us to make a promise; we have to take a stand. Our first step is to hang the scarlet cord on the door of our heart by accepting Christ as our Savior. When we choose to say "yes" to the kindness of God, He pulls us out of our Jericho places that try to drag us toward destruction. And it's a "yes" that's more than a word: it's a life that demonstrates real faith. Disobedience tries to derail our destiny, one choice at a time. But obedience opens the door to opportunity when we give faith space to breathe.

Find Your Fearless

FEARLESS TAKEAWAY

Kindness is the vehicle that transports favor.

FEARLESS NEXT STEPS

1. Obedience opens the door to opportunity when we give faith space to breathe. Our first step is to hang the scarlet cord on the door of our heart by accepting Christ as our Savior. If you have never said "yes" to Jesus' invitation, now is your moment to receive His grace and mercy.

2. In 2 Samuel 9, we witness a stunning example of kindness on display. "Seeking out one of Saul's servants, Ziba, David asked, "Is there no one still alive from the house of Saul to whom I can show God's kindness?"" Consider ways God might be asking you to show kindness this week, especially to someone who hurt you.

3. Rahab wasn't foolish; she was fearless. Think about a current situation requiring action on your part. Ask the Holy Spirit to help you discern the right steps to take in the days ahead to protect the integrity of your choices.

FEARLESS DECLARATION

I choose to hang the scarlet cord of salvation on the door of my heart. I accept Christ as my Savior, recognizing there is nothing I could do to earn grace. I will to let kindness govern my actions. I will give faith space to breathe and walk through God's open doors of opportunity.

FEARLESS PRAYER

My prayer in my words…

Her Catalyst for Change—Stand Strong

As the men disappeared into the darkness, Rahab dared to make a choice that changed history. However, her swift action was followed by silence. Waiting is never easy, especially when your life is hanging in the balance. While Rahab patiently held on to faith, God put pieces in place on the other side of the wall.

Let's pick up our story again in Joshua 2:22: "When they left, they went into the hills and stayed there three days, until the pursuers had searched all along the road and returned without finding them. Then the two men started back. They went down out of the hills, forded the river and came to Joshua son of Nun and told him everything that had happened to them. They said to Joshua, "The Lord has surely given the whole land into our hands; all the people are melting in fear because of us."

In the days that followed, God prepared the Israelites for the colossal task ahead. As they carried the Ark of the Covenant, signifying the presence of God, God miraculously parted the waters of the Jordan River enabling them to cross on dry land. As they set up memorial stones to commemorate the moment, God asked them to renew their commitment through circumcision. And as they neared Jericho, God gave them the battle plan.

Joshua 6: 2 "Then the Lord said to Joshua, "See, I have delivered Jericho into your hands, along with its king and its fighting men. March around the city once with all the armed men. Do this for six days. Have seven priests carry trumpets of rams' horns in front of the ark. On the seventh day, march around the city seven times, with the priests blowing the trumpets. When you hear them sound a long blast on the trumpets, have the whole army give a loud shout; then the wall of the city will collapse and the army will go up, everyone straight in"."

For six consecutive days, the Israelite army meticulously followed God's orders, marching around the walls of Jericho by day and camping by night. Don't you wonder what the inhabitants of Jericho thought? After all, this was unlike any military approach anyone had ever seen. With bated breath and barred gates, a city hunkered in fear. Except Rahab.

How her heart must have leapt as the sound of footsteps finally broke through the quiet night air. She too had been preparing. She was determined to leave, all right, and she wasn't leaving alone. Although we aren't privy to the conversations that took place between her and her family, just imagine the intense discussion. Lean in as she describes in vivid detail the night the spies visited her home. Listen closely as she pleads with them to trust her with their lives. Love her for her fearless tenacity that persuades every member of her family to follow her to freedom. Because of her obedience and willingness to stand out, her home became a sanctuary for the deliverance of her entire family.

Daybreak announced the dawn of the seventh day, and the Israelite army began to circle the city of Jericho. Not once. Not twice. Seven times. And on the seventh time around, Joshua commanded the army: "Shout! For the Lord has given you the city! The city and all that is in it are to be devoted to the Lord. Only Rahab the prostitute and all who are with her in her house shall be spared, because she hid the spies we sent."

> As trumpet blasts and thunderous shouts split the sky, Rahab held fast to her mother's arm. It was all happening so fast...the deafening roar of a city under siege...the whoosh of the men rushing past her...and in mere seconds... the wall around her collapsed into rubble. She squeezed her eyes shut and struggled to take a breath in the billowing dust.
>
> "Rahab!"
>
> In an instant, she knew their voices—and she knew she was safe.

"So the young men who had done the spying went in and brought out Rahab, her father and mother, her brothers and sisters and all who belonged to her. They brought out her entire family and put them in a place outside the camp of Israel. Then they burned the whole city and everything in it, but they put the silver and gold and the articles of bronze and iron into the treasury of the Lord's house. But Joshua spared Rahab the prostitute, with her family and all who belonged to her, because she hid the men Joshua had sent as spies to Jericho—and she lives among the Israelites to this day."

While everything she knew crumbled around her, Rahab stood strong. This seemingly ordinary woman distinguished herself through her extraordinary kindness and faith. She lied for the spies, protected the spies, and left with the spies. Faith enabled her to turn away from the lure of her culture and turn toward a life of purpose. She is the antithesis of Lot's wife, a woman caught in a similar situation, who *didn't* want to leave. Genesis 19 shares the story of Sodom and Gomorrah, a wicked city destined for destruction. Because of Lot's relationship with Abraham, angelic messengers warned him and his family about the impending devastation. Despite a merciful offer of escape, Lot hesitated.

Verse 16: "When he hesitated, the men grasped his hand and the hands of his wife and of his two daughters and led them safely out of the city, for the Lord was merciful to them. As soon as they had brought them out, one of them said, "Flee for your lives! Don't look back, and don't stop anywhere in the plain! Flee to the mountains or you will be swept away!"

By the time Lot reached Zoar, the sun had risen over the land. Then the Lord rained down burning sulfur on Sodom and Gomorrah—from the Lord out of the heavens. Thus he overthrew those cities and the entire plain, destroying all those living in the cities—and also the vegetation in the land. But Lot's wife looked back, and she became a pillar of salt."

Girls, these two women stand in stark contrast with one another, each a signpost to us today. One couldn't escape her past and one refused to be defined by it. Lot's wife serves as a reminder of the dangers we face when we hold on to sin or refuse to let go of the things that keep us in bondage. The last thing the enemy wants is for us to stand strong as women who fearlessly follow God. He wields three powerful weapons to keep us from moving forward in our calling:

Shame keeps us imprisoned by our former choices or lifestyle.
Insecurity tempts us to doubt ourselves or God's faithfulness.
Anxiety entices us to look backwards out of fear of the future.

Any of these missiles could've easily derailed Rahab's destiny. Yet, she disarmed each attack as she placed her faith in God. She was liberated from her past and freed to step into her future.

Rahab's life points us to grace. **Grace is the undoing of something old and the unfolding of something new.** It is the awareness that God picks us up out of the rubble and leads us to safety. It is the realization that God longs to save us, redeem us, and use us. It is the promise that we will no longer remain paralyzed by our past, but we will walk fearlessly into all that lies ahead. And if we look closely enough, we might just trace Rahab's footsteps. Her story didn't end in the outskirts of a camp; it had only just begun.

Sometimes—no, most times, God's plans don't look anything like ours. This nail-biter of a rescue story was God's design all along. He isn't the tiniest bit intimidated by sin, and He chose a woman who wasn't the tiniest bit intimidated by circumstances. Rahab committed herself to the Israelites before she gained possession of the land. She identified with them when they had nothing but God. She stayed strong while they scrapped every plausible military strategy to implement a plan completely contingent on faith. Her actions became the catalyst that changed the lives of many. And God rewarded her by engrafting her into the Jewish nation. Matthew 1 tells us that she was adopted into the faith as the first Gentile convert. She became the wife of Salmon and the mother of Boaz, putting her in direct lineage to Jesus.

Rahab, praised throughout Scripture for her fearless faith, is last mentioned in Hebrews. Hebrews 11 contains a list of some of the most remarkable men and women in the Bible: Abraham, Moses, Joseph, Moses' parents, and David, just to name a few. And there—taking her place alongside other ordinary heroes who dared to do extraordinary things—is Rahab. Verse 31: "By faith the prostitute Rahab, because she welcomed the spies, was not killed with those who were disobedient."

This is what happens when God intersects our story with grace.

Find Your Fearless

FEARLESS TAKEAWAY

Grace is the undoing of something old and the unfolding of something new.

FEARLESS NEXT STEPS

1. Because of her obedience and willingness to stand out, Rahab's home became a sanctuary for the deliverance of her entire family. How can your home serve as a place of hope and healing?

2. Genesis 19 shares the story of Sodom and Gomorrah, a wicked city destined for destruction. Lot's wife serves as a reminder of the dangers we face when we hold on to sin or refuse to let go of the past. Take a moment to identify any area where you're tempted to look back and surrender it to the Lord.

3. The enemy wields three powerful weapons to keep us from moving forward in our calling: shame, insecurity, and anxiety. Which tends to trip you up? Allow God to intersect those places with His grace.

FEARLESS DECLARATION

I will make my home a place of hope and healing for my family and others who enter her walls. I surrender any area of my past seeking to hold me back from God's purposes for my life. I embrace the unfolding of something new in me as grace wins the battle for my heart. I will choose gratitude every day because God chose me to be His own.

FEARLESS PRAYER

My prayer in my words...

Her Calling and Ours

Moxie. Webster's dictionary defines it as "fortitude and determination," but it's just as easily summed up in one word: Rahab. Despite her sordid past, the call of God on her life made her fearless. This ordinary woman, shunned by her culture and poised for annihilation, was miraculously spared because of her audacious faith. She dared to believe that her life—and the life of her family—was worth saving. She was willing to sacrifice herself to cooperate with God because she understood a secret: sin is no match for grace.

The ink on the pages of Scripture scribbles this message across our delicate hearts: our past doesn't have to paralyze our future. Many of us flinch when someone attempts to dig up something we've painstakingly buried under a mound of dirt and debris. As much as we long to climb out of the rubble, we're just not sure we're strong enough to pick up a shovel.

Others of us don't struggle with what's behind us, but we do worry if we're up to what's in front of us. Walls of doubt loom ominously over the promise of our destiny. Our hopeful "yes," bursting with expectancy, becomes muted by uncertainty.

But will I ever get out from under my past?
But am I talented enough to do this?
But will I be a good mom?
But will my new business venture be a disaster?
But will my cancer return?

But what if we stopped hiding? What if we, instead, decided to stake our life on the scarlet cord of redemption? Rahab's story inspires us to gather our grit and grab ahold of our future. This epic tale of rescue and restoration sheds valuable light on the path ahead—both for us individually, and for our culture. When we exercise our faith, we overcome obstacles and encounter an extraordinary God.

TEAR DOWN WALLS

Emerging from a painful past or engaging with an unknown future can seem daunting. Yet it's possible to thaw out from the deep freeze of fear. As women, we're strangely deft at building walls to hide our brokenness. We build barriers to guard ourselves from the pain of criticism and comparison. We keep others at arm's length, afraid of letting people truly know us. After all, it feels safer behind a screen than in front of a crowd. We can text or type without the danger of intimacy. But that, dear friends, is no way to live.

When sin entered the Garden of Eden, Adam and Eve's initial instinct was to hide. They disobeyed God by taking a bite of forbidden fruit and experienced the bitter taste of shame for the first time. They desperately wanted to cover it up, sewing together fig leaves and trying to disappear from the presence of God. When God called for Adam, he answered in Genesis 3:10: "I heard you in the garden, and I was afraid because I was naked; so I hid."

Guilt. Fear. Separation. Nothing would ever be the same. God knew their best efforts would never suffice; this required a sacrifice. God Himself made garments for Adam and Eve, clothing them with the skin of an animal He created. His plan to rescue, redeem, and restore mankind demanded the sacrifice of His Son, Jesus. The blood of Jesus covers our sin—and our shame. He not only forgives our sin, He takes the pain and heartbreak we were never intended to carry.

No matter what our past, God can redeem us and use us. He doesn't want any of us suffering in the shadow of shame or haunted by regret. He wants to clothe us with a new identity and the knowledge that we are deeply valued and dearly loved. When we're confident in who we are in Christ, we are far less likely to crouch behind the wall of comparison. When we begin comparing ourselves to others instead of cementing our worth in Christ, we question if we truly belong. Rahab found her place of belonging when she chose to identify herself with the people of God. She embraced a completely new way of living.

Girls, let's stop living on islands of isolation because we're threatened by criticism and competition. Let's look out from behind our walls and see all the women who need our stories. Jesus handed us the scarlet rope of redemption. Now, stand up, stand strong, and throw that rope to a sister who needs you to help pull her out of the rubble.

TEAR OFF LABELS

Rahab lived in a sexually explicit society, just as we do today. Women in the United States, and around the world, face constant temptation and pressure from highly sexualized cultures. How do we choose to honor God with our bodies while the world continually places our bodies on show? As I studied the disturbing statistics involving sexual activity, sexual violence, prostitution, and abortion, my heart hurt. I've sat across dinner tables with precious friends as they processed deep regret. I've cried at altars with women as they struggled to forgive the unthinkable. I've led worship with survivors of sex trafficking as they pressed into God for healing. Only Jesus can tear off these labels...

- Among unmarried 15–19-year-olds, 44% of females and 49% of males had had sexual intercourse.[9]
- From 1973 through 2011, nearly 53 million legal abortions occurred in the United States. In 2014, approximately 19% of U.S. pregnancies (excluding spontaneous miscarriages) ended in abortion.[10]
- Every 92 seconds, an American is sexually assaulted. And every 9 minutes, that victim is a child. 1 out of every 6 American women has been the victim of an attempted or completed rape in her lifetime. Meanwhile, only 5 out of every 1,000 perpetrators will end up in prison.
- One in four girls and one in six boys will be sexually abused before they turn 18 years old.
- Victims of sexual violence suffer long-term effects including PTSD, depression, and suicidal thoughts. People who have been sexually

assaulted are more likely to use drugs than the general public and experience increased problems in relationships with their family, friends and co-workers.[11]

- Worldwide, there is an estimation of 40–42 million prostitutes. Eighty percent of the world's population of prostitutes are female and range in age between 13–25. While these statistics about prostitution are just touching the surface, they indicate the extent of the sex-for-sale industry worldwide.[12]

This list is disorienting. Overwhelming. Because behind every number is a face: a young girl with a bright future…a scared college student with an unplanned pregnancy…a hardened abuse victim turned prostitute. And what do we do? We slap labels—on ourselves, and on others.

Labels that say:

Broken.
Shattered.
Ruined.

Perhaps you've worn a label. Or perhaps someone you love is counted in the dizzying list of records above. And we think: *"I'm too _____ for God to use me."* We impose limitations on God, convinced that choices we've made will keep God from loving us—or wanting us. Rahab knew the familiar smack of a label. She had worn them all her life. In fact, even the books of James and Hebrews refer to her as "the prostitute," "the harlot", Rahab. However, they do this not as a means of parading her past, but as a platform to exhibit grace.

Rahab let grace tear off the labels. She refused to allow anything to diminish her value to the kingdom of God. No matter what we have done, or what has been done to us, nothing can keep God from using us. God will use the worst of circumstances to bring out the best in us. He can heal any wound, right any wrong, and tear off any label.

God sees you. You matter. You are not the identity the world brands on you when you encounter Christ. He removes the residue stuck to our hearts and peels off the lies affixed to our minds. **Labels were made for packages, not people.** When we find our identity in Christ and know who we are in Him, we wear a new kind of label:

Chosen.
Called.
Loved.

Do you see it? From the moment Eve's lips touched that apple, God initiated His plan of redemption. And we, girls, we find our fearless in Him.

TEAR OFF A NEW PAGE

Rahab is a beautiful picture of the relationship between our loving Heavenly Father and the bride of Christ. God specializes in rescue, redemption, and restoration. Perhaps someone you love refuses to tear off a label. Don't give up on them. Keep praying, reaching out, and anticipating walls to fall as you step out in faith. You just never know which lap you're marching on in your journey around Jericho.

We, too, can tear off a new page. When we allow God to excavate the painful places of our lives, we can walk boldly in our calling. We don't have to fear the future. God is fighting for you, going before you, and making the way straight. When we least expect it, God intersects our story with grace. And when He does, there's no looking back. We'll take every regret and turn it into fuel. We'll get unstuck from shame and share our story. We'll watch in awe as our worship tears down walls. And when they fall, we'll shout even louder because we know what it feels like to be free.

Find Your Fearless

FEARLESS TAKEAWAY

Labels are made for packages, not people.

FEARLESS NEXT STEPS

1. Sometimes walls of doubt loom ominously over the promise of our destiny. Our hopeful "yes," bursting with expectancy, becomes muted by uncertainty. Is there any area you need God to equip you with "Holy Spirit moxie?"

2. As women, we often build barriers to guard ourselves from the pain of criticism and comparison. Where do you tend to barricade yourself behind a wall? Who might need you to come out of hiding and throw them a rope?

3. When we wear the world's labels, we impose limitations on God, convinced that choices we've made will keep God from loving us—or wanting us. And we think: "I'm too _____ for God to use me." How might you fill in the blank? How can you replace that with the truth of how God sees you?

FEARLESS DECLARATION

I will no longer struggle with what lies behind me or before me. I will allow grace to tear off every label and give me the strength to share my story. I will not stop praying for those I love, believing that they will see themselves the way God sees them. I will live every day astounded that I am chosen. I am called. I am loved.

FEARLESS PRAYER

My prayer in my words…

Abigail

Her Story & Our Starting Place

> We can seize the moment when
> we know the mind of God.

1 SAMUEL 25

Before you begin your study, view the companion video resource here:

 | www.angeladonadio.com

I have also included the video message and our key Scripture passage below.

\\|/

Welcome to Session 3! I hope you're loving getting to know these ordinary, but fearless, women of the Bible. God wants us to find our fearless in their stories. Today, we move forward hundreds of years, about 1000 years before the birth of Christ. After Joshua's death, the Israelites went through a time of leadership by the judges, followed by a newly established political system with Saul as king. In our previous session, we were briefly introduced to Saul and his successor, David. As Saul slid tragically into failure, God asked Samuel the prophet to anoint David as king. This enraged Saul, who still held the position. Eaten alive by jealousy, Saul hunted David and his rag-tag army of 600 men through desert caves and strongholds. In that area, they served as defenders of the men and flocks belonging to a wealthy landowner, Nabal. David sent messengers to ask for favor and supplies in return for their protection. But the wicked, unmanageable Nabal refused, angering David to the point of retaliation.

At a critical moment in David's life, when his choices threatened to derail his destiny, God intervened through Nabal's wife, Abigail. She was the whole package, girls: beauty and brains, wisdom and willingness. But she was married to a total jerk, and completely unaware of how God planned to use her. She rose above her difficult home life and miserable circumstances to head off danger, just in the nick of time.

Live From En Gedi ◇◇◇◇◇◇◇◇◇◇◇◇◇◇◇

I'm in beautiful En Gedi. It's here that Abigail's quick thinking and intervention redirected David and diffused a potentially disastrous situation for all involved. She saddled up her donkey near this place and rode into the ravine, risking her life to plead with a furious David and his armed men. She seized the moment because she understood the mind of God. Let's read her story in 1 Samuel 25. We'll see right away that David's pastor and friend, the prophet Samuel, died, and God raised up Abigail within the same passage of Scripture to pick up the torch and speak life into David when he needed it most.

1 Samuel 25.

"Now Samuel died, and all Israel assembled and mourned for him; and they buried him at his home in Ramah. Then David moved down into the Desert of Paran.

A certain man in Maon, who had property there at Carmel, was very wealthy. He had a thousand goats and three thousand sheep, which he was shearing in Carmel. His name was Nabal and his wife's name was Abigail. She was an intelligent and beautiful woman, but her husband was surly and mean in his dealings—he was a Calebite.

While David was in the wilderness, he heard that Nabal was shearing sheep. So he sent ten young men and said to them, "Go up to Nabal at Carmel and greet him in my name. Say to him: 'Long life to you! Good health to you and your household! And good health to all that is yours!

"'Now I hear that it is sheep-shearing time. When your shepherds were with us, we did not mistreat them, and the whole time they were at Carmel nothing of theirs was missing. Ask your own servants and they will tell you. Therefore, be favorable toward my men, since we come at a festive time. Please give your servants and your son David whatever you can find for them.'"

When David's men arrived, they gave Nabal this message in David's name. Then they waited.

Nabal answered David's servants, "Who is this David? Who is this son of Jesse? Many servants are breaking away from their masters these days. Why should I take my bread and water, and the meat I have slaughtered for my shearers, and give it to men coming from who knows where?"

David's men turned around and went back. When they arrived, they reported every word. David said to his men, "Each of you strap on your sword!" So they did, and David strapped his on as well.

About four hundred men went up with David, while two hundred stayed with the supplies.

One of the servants told Abigail, Nabal's wife, "David sent messengers from the wilderness to give our master his greetings, but he hurled insults at them. Yet these men were very good to us. They did not mistreat us, and the whole time we were out in the fields near them nothing was missing. Night and day they were a wall around us the whole time we were herding our sheep near them. Now think it over and see what you can do, because disaster is hanging over our master and his whole household. He is such a wicked man that no one can talk to him."

Abigail acted quickly. She took two hundred loaves of bread, two skins of wine, five dressed sheep, five seahs of roasted grain, a hundred cakes of raisins and two hundred cakes of pressed figs, and loaded them on donkeys. Then she told her servants, "Go on ahead; I'll follow you." But she did not tell her husband Nabal.

As she came riding her donkey into a mountain ravine, there were David and his men descending toward her, and she met them. David had just said, "It's been useless—all my watching over this fellow's property in the wilderness so that nothing of his was missing. He has paid me back evil for good. May God deal with David, be it ever so severely, if by morning I leave alive one male of all who belong to him!"

When Abigail saw David, she quickly got off her donkey and bowed down before David with her face to the ground. She fell at his feet and said: "Pardon your servant, my lord, and let me speak to you; hear what your servant has to say. Please pay no attention, my lord, to that wicked man Nabal. He is just like his name—his name means Fool, and folly goes with him. And as for me, your servant, I did not see the men my lord sent. And now, my lord, as surely as the Lord your God lives and as you live, since the Lord has kept you from bloodshed and from avenging yourself with your own hands, may your enemies and all who are intent on harming my lord be like Nabal. And let this gift, which your servant has brought to my lord, be given to the men who follow you.

"Please forgive your servant's presumption. The Lord your God will certainly make a lasting dynasty for my lord, because you fight the Lord's battles, and no wrongdoing will be found in you as long as you live. Even though someone is pursuing you to take your life, the life of my lord will be bound securely in the bundle of the living by the Lord your God, but the lives of your enemies he will hurl away as from the pocket of a sling. When the Lord has fulfilled for my lord every good thing he promised concerning him and has appointed him ruler over Israel, my lord will not have on his conscience the staggering burden of needless bloodshed or of having avenged himself. And when the Lord your God has brought my lord success, remember your servant."

David said to Abigail, "Praise be to the Lord, the God of Israel, who has sent you today to meet me. May you be blessed for your good judgment and for keeping me from bloodshed this day and from avenging myself with my own hands. Otherwise, as surely as the Lord, the God of Israel, lives, who has kept me from harming you, if you had not come quickly to meet me, not one male belonging to Nabal would have been left alive by daybreak."

Then David accepted from her hand what she had brought him and said, "Go home in peace. I have heard your words and granted your request."

When Abigail went to Nabal, he was in the house holding a banquet like that of a king. He was in high spirits and very drunk. So she told him nothing at all until daybreak. Then in the morning, when Nabal was sober, his wife told him all these things, and his heart failed him and he became like a stone. About ten days later, the LORD struck Nabal and he died.

When David heard that Nabal was dead, he said, "Praise be to the LORD, who has upheld my cause against Nabal for treating me with contempt. He has kept his servant from doing wrong and has brought Nabal's wrongdoing down on his own head."

Then David sent word to Abigail, asking her to become his wife. His servants went to Carmel and said to Abigail, "David has sent us to you to take you to become his wife."

She bowed down with her face to the ground and said, "I am your servant and am ready to serve you and wash the feet of my lord's servants." Abigail quickly got on a donkey and, attended by her five female servants, went with David's messengers and became his wife. David had also married Ahinoam of Jezreel, and they both were his wives. But Saul had given his daughter Michal, David's wife, to Paltiel son of Laish, who was from Gallim.

I don't know about you, but my heart would've been racing riding down that ravine, not knowing how this thing was going to turn out. I'm not sure donkeys can race...and I'm not about to find out. But Abigail? She's fearless, placing her confidence fully in God. Because she's willing to stand up and stand out, God used her as a catalyst for change. Girls, you can seize the moment when you know the mind of God.

◇◇

It was no small hike up to the top to view that spectacular waterfall. As I squeezed through passageways and scrambled over rocks, I imagined the fierce determination that drove Abigail to action. Understanding the urgency of the situation, she loaded up her donkey with supplies and steadied her heart with purpose.

Her faith propelled her to disarm an explosive situation. She delivered a feast for a king, and much-needed peace. Our words can bring healing into overheated places when we carry wisdom and humility.

Abigail's ability to seize the moment inspires us to make culture-shaping choices. It doesn't matter how bad your situation looks, or what you're walking into. God goes before you and He can use you to be an instrument of His mercy when you're willing to act in faith.

We can SEIZE THE MOMENT *when we know the mind of God.*

Her Cause—Stand Up

Abigail took the last loaf out of the oven and dusted the flour from her linen tunic. The rich aromas of freshly baked bread and sweet figs wafted from her kitchen, awakening her senses and lifting her spirits. Her eyes scanned the familiar landscape of the room where she had so often sought solace. She felt the corners of her mouth curl into a gentle smile as she reflected on this place of respite. It seemed like ages since she had first stepped onto the grounds of this large estate. In those early days following her arranged marriage, the magnitude of it all seemed overwhelming. But now, she relished the opportunity to oversee so many details and protect the people under her care. This wasn't the life she had dreamt of, but she had made the most of it.

A knock at the door jarred her back into the present moment. As soon as she saw her servant's face, she knew something was terribly wrong. As he described the impending catastrophe, Abigail's heart sank.

"Disaster is hanging over our master and our whole household. We didn't know what else to do but come to you. He's such a wicked man...you know none of us can talk to him."

His words confirmed her worst fears. She felt her knees buckle as she propped herself up against the counter. *"Think, Abigail,"* she chided herself. And the answer came.

"I know he's unreasonable, but I never thought it would get this bad. Get the servants to load a caravan of donkeys with food. I'll be right behind you. Hurry!"

Abigail's prudent action halted the collision course prompted by her husband's poor choices and David's frustrations. Cross a wicked landowner with an exasperated outlaw on the run from a crazed king, and you've got the makings of a major battle. Little did she know that her quick thinking would prevent David from falling into the same trap that haunted Saul. She bolstered him to keep his sword clean and taught him a lesson he didn't forget. Let's learn a little more about our leading men, David and Nabal.

In three successive passages of Scripture, David faced three personal tests. Each time, he was placed in a position of power with an opportunity to use it for personal ends. In 1 Samuel chapters 24 and 26, David exercised great restraint, sparing Saul's life when he had not one, but two, chances to take it. Nestled between these accounts is the story that catapulted Abigail to center stage.

David, on the run from Saul, moved down to the desert of Moan on the southern border of the Sinai wilderness. He and his men protected the sheep in nearby areas—including those owned by Nabal—from Bedouins and wild animals. During sheep-shearing, a time of open-handed hospitality among flock masters, David sent 10 young men to bring a greeting and blessing to Nabal. They explained how they had graciously taken care of his flocks and servants, fully expecting gratitude and provisions in return.

1 Samuel 25:7 shares, 'When your shepherds were with us, we did not mistreat them, and the whole time they were at Carmel nothing of theirs was missing. Ask your own servants and they will tell you. Therefore, be favorable toward my men, since we come at a festive time. Please give your servants and your son David whatever you can find for them.'

When David's men arrived, they gave Nabal this message in David's name. Then they waited.

Nabal answered David's servants, "Who is this David? Who is this son of Jesse? Many servants are breaking away from their masters these days. Why should I take my bread and water, and the meat I have slaughtered for my shearers, and give it to men coming from who knows where?"

Yep. Them are fightin' words. Tired, hungry, and sick of his conditions, David hoped for a much more favorable response. However, if he had known Nabal, he wouldn't have been surprised. Nabal "son of Belial," literally means a beast of a man. Verse 3 describes him as "mean and surly in all his dealings, a Calebite." This tells us he was a corrupt man who deviated from a family line of those who knew the history of the Israelites. Abandoning any ties to faith, his personality dossier reveals a deadly combination: rude, rich, brutal, drunk, unmanageable, stubborn, and ill-tempered. Yikes.

Although he knew David, and certainly had the means to reward him, he ignored him and insulted him. Disregarding David's protection, he was stingy, ungrateful, and selfish. When the abysmal report reached David's ears, he and 400 men reached for their swords. Thankfully, word got to Abigail in time. Although both Nabal and Abigail knew about David, they reacted in completely different ways to the information. Although Scripture doesn't share much about her background, we see that she understood current world events and managed a large household that held her in high esteem.

Right off the bat, 1 Samuel 25 shares two of her standout qualities: she was beautiful and intelligent. Perhaps her character went overlooked by her coarse husband, but not by others. As news of the imminent conflict spread, one of the servants brought the information directly to Abigail. He demonstrated full confidence in her character, trusting she would consider the facts and handle the situation with diplomacy and wisdom.

And that she did. It wasn't the first time she had been employed to serve as the peace-maker in this home. She was hardly a novice at navigating the choppy waters of living with a difficult person. She knew the futility of attempting a rational conversation with an irrational person. She knew this called for action.

Strategically poised between two opposing parties giving in to their inflated emotions, she simultaneously protected them both. She stood up to fight for the cause of David's integrity and her husband's life. She refused to let wearisome circumstances define her. She used what she had—her words—to save her entire household and rescue David from himself.

And girls, she did it quickly. She made a split-second decision to intervene, putting herself right in the middle of the fight. She could've walked away…let someone else deal with it this time. But not Abigail. In the eye of a tornado of so much going wrong, she collected the strength to stand up and do what was right.

It's not easy when we find ourselves smack dab in the middle of a difficult situation. Abigail gets it—and she has a lot more to teach us than her recipe for lentil stew. She recognizes the temptation to take the easy way out. She understands the pull to choose comfort over the challenge of a cause. But she knows that when we remain silent when God calls us to speak up, we abdicate our responsibility.

Fear tells us to be quiet in the face of gross injustice.
Mediocrity keeps us from speaking out when our voice is desperately needed.
Indifference lets someone else take the wheel while we take a backseat.

But that tense work environment, that heated conversation, that inexcusable grievance—is asking for you.

Our next step might not involve saddling up a donkey, but it will involve faith. Hebrews 11:1 describes faith this way: "Now faith is confidence in what we hope for and assurance about what we do not see." When we don't know what we're walking—or riding—into, faith is our guide. The more we trust the character of God and know His heart in a situation, the more we'll act in confidence. We strengthen our faith and develop our ability to recognize His voice as we spend time in His Word and His presence. Our actions, then, are based on truth and not raw emotion. His Word protects us when the world prods us to be rash.

What unhinged situation needs your voice? Believe you can make a difference. Start by refusing to play it safe and seize that God-moment. It will require us to take an honest look at places we've become numb to the need around us. It will involve us doing our part so God will do His. **Fear steers us to settle, but faith drives us to dare.** So, grab those reins girls, and let's ride alongside Abigail. But wait. What can one woman do against a sea of armed men? Why, I'm so glad you asked.

Find Your Fearless

FEARLESS TAKEAWAY

Fear steers us to settle, but faith drives us to dare.

FEARLESS NEXT STEPS

1. Strategically poised between two opposing parties giving in to their inflated emotions, Abigail simultaneously protected them both. She refused to be defined by wearisome circumstances and used what she had—her words. Can you relate to Abigail's dilemma? If so, what God-given attribute can you use to benefit all parties involved?

2. Fear tells us to be quiet in the face of gross injustice. Mediocrity keeps us from speaking out when our voice is desperately needed. Indifference lets someone else take the wheel while we take a back seat. Which one of these three areas—fear, mediocrity, or indifference—pose a temptation for you? How do the words of Hebrews 11:1 draw you out of areas of complacency?

3. What unhinged situation needs your voice? How can you use your words to bring healing and peace?

FEARLESS DECLARATION

I will not let fear silence my voice. I refuse to choose mediocrity when God is calling me to act. I will take an honest look at any area I've become indifferent to the needs around me. I will seize the God-moments to make a difference in the lives of others.

FEARLESS PRAYER

My prayer in my words…

Her Choice—Stand Out

Abigail barreled into the ravine, racing against the clock to reach David before it was too late. She was careful, however, not to leave without her tried and true travel companion: wisdom. It's not enough to be quick on our feet. We need to marry action with wisdom.

What is wisdom? Webster's dictionary defines it as, "the trait of utilizing knowledge and experience with common sense and insight." James 1:5 tells us how to access wisdom. "If any of you lacks wisdom, you should ask God, who gives generously to all without finding fault, and it will be given to you."

James continues in Chapter 3:17–18 to define godly wisdom this way: "But the wisdom that comes from heaven is first of all pure; then peace-loving, considerate, submissive, full of mercy and good fruit, impartial and sincere. Peacemakers who sow in peace reap a harvest of righteousness." *This* is the perfect picture of Abigail.

Wisdom counseled her to not say a word to Nabal. Girls, not everything warrants public consumption. When God is using you, sometimes it's best to keep it under wraps so He can work and receive the glory.

Wisdom rushed her out the door. Once the problem presented itself, Abigail lost no time. When God speaks, we need to act, not saunter around waiting for somebody else to show up. **Sometimes we are the solution.**

Wisdom advised her to gather food and provisions for David and his tired, hungry, thirsty, disgruntled, (need I go on?) men. Our woman of the hour showed up with 200 loaves of bread, 2 skins of wine (each carrying many gallons), 5 dressed sheep (ready to eat), 5 seahs of roasted grain (60 pounds), 100 cakes of raisins, and 200 cakes of pressed figs. (Good grief; did she already have all this food cooked?)

And wisdom guided her to judiciously wield her words, disarming 400 men ready to wield their weapons. Let's rejoin Abigail's story in 1 Samuel 25:20:

> "As she came riding her donkey into a mountain ravine, there were David and his men descending toward her, and she met them. David had just said, "It's been useless—all my watching over this fellow's property in the wilderness so that nothing of his was missing. He has paid me back evil for good. May God deal with David, be it ever so severely, if by morning I leave alive one male of all who belong to him!""

David's anger and utter exasperation reached a boiling point, culminating in three telling words: "It's been useless." Ever been there? Ever watched as God promised something, yet all your effort seemed worthless? Ever wondered if there was a point in serving God when nothing turned out the way you hoped? Yeah, me too. Those sacred spaces when we throw off the down comforter of safety for the downpour of sacrifice can become fertile ground for disappointment. The enemy wants us to believe that we seized a God-moment in vain.

We prayed for our children every day only for them to make destructive choices anyway. We stayed with our spouse through the valley only for him to leave after all. We made a real effort to befriend that group of women only for them to talk about us behind our backs. People's hurtful reactions to our best efforts sting. And unmet expectations leave a mark. Yet faith bleeds onto the page of our disappointment and shows us that nothing was wasted. Faith redirects our feelings to the truth of God's Word and reminds us of our worth in Him.

And sometimes, when we are in danger from our flesh, God raises up someone to intervene. God uses situations to warn us and sends people to rescue us. As David struggled to maintain his equilibrium, Abigail put herself in danger to stop him from toppling over. With all the excitement of an action movie, she showed up just as David finished breathing out threats. In stark contrast to Nabal, whose words added fuel to the fire, Abigail's words took the heat out of the situation.

"When Abigail saw David, she quickly got off her donkey and bowed down before David with her face to the ground. She fell at his feet and said: "Pardon your servant, my lord, and let me speak to you; hear what your servant has to say. Please pay no attention, my lord, to that wicked man Nabal. He is just like his name—his name means Fool, and folly goes with him. And as for me, your servant, I did not see the men my lord sent. And now, my lord, as surely as the Lord your God lives and as you live, since the Lord has kept you from bloodshed and from avenging yourself with your own hands, may your enemies and all who are intent on harming my lord be like Nabal. And let this gift, which your servant has brought to my lord, be given to the men who follow you.

"Please forgive your servant's presumption. The Lord your God will certainly make a lasting dynasty for my lord, because you fight the Lord's battles, and no wrongdoing will be found in you as long as you live. Even though someone is pursuing you to take your life, the life of my lord will be bound securely in the bundle of the living by the Lord your God, but the lives of your enemies he will hurl away as from the pocket of a sling. When the Lord has fulfilled for my lord every good thing he promised concerning him and has appointed him ruler over Israel, my lord will not have on his conscience the staggering burden of needless bloodshed or of having avenged himself. And when the Lord your God has brought my lord success, remember your servant.""

Good. Ness. That was a speech. Let's break it down into bite-size pieces so we don't miss a thing.

In humility and honor, she fell facedown before David. *Wisdom.* "A Hebrew woman was restricted by the customs of her time to give counsel only in an emergency and in the hour of greatest need. Abigail, who had risked the displeasure of her husband, whose life was threatened, did not act impulsively in going to David to plead for mercy."[13]

She requested a chance to speak and asked him to listen. She apologized for the actions of her husband and let him know that if she had spoken to his men, she would've handled it differently. *Wisdom.*

She then proceeded to string together several key statements that make an obvious point: ***"You, David, are the divinely appointed king."*** And with assurance that only comes from God, she stepped into her calling.

> *"David, this is not your fight. You fight the Lord's battles, and that's another level all together. You have the heart of God and your integrity is worth saving. And when you're king—and you will be—you won't carry the staggering burden of needless bloodshed. David, avoid this trap of the enemy and go on to blessing. And when you do, remember me." Wisdom.*

Her calm soothed David's chaos. She seized her moment because she knew the mind of God. David recognized this was a divine appointment and prayed a blessing over her life for intervening in his. He conveyed with honesty that her choices saved many lives. Because of her willingness to stand out, she became a catalyst for change.

"David said to Abigail, "Praise be to the Lord, the God of Israel, who has sent you today to meet me. May you be blessed for your good judgment and for keeping me from bloodshed this day and from avenging myself with my own hands. Otherwise, as surely as the Lord, the God of Israel, lives, who has kept me from harming you, if you had not come quickly to meet me, not one male belonging to Nabal would have been left alive by daybreak." Then David accepted from her hand what she had brought him and said, "Go home in peace. I have heard your words and granted your request.""

Our words matter. They carry the power to diffuse a bomb or detonate one. We never know how our words and actions may affect others. Wisdom walks us through these questions before we speak:

> *Does it need to be said?*
> *When should it be said?*
> *How should it be said?*

As we filter every decision through the lens of wisdom, we bring peace into potentially explosive situations. When God is asking us to act, we shouldn't hesitate to be an agent of change, even when risk is involved. When we know the mind of God, we can seize God-moments with confidence.

As quickly as Abigail had arrived on the scene, she returned home. Her faithfulness, self-control, kindness, common sense, and vision—all bathed in wisdom—made her fearless. She was the perfect candidate for God to use as an instrument of His mercy. She separated herself completely from the spirit of Nabal while being loyal to him. She risked her life and dared to confront a would-be king with no strings attached. She made the right choice because it was the right choice, not because she carried an ultimatum. And we'll soon see how God honored her faith.

Find Your Fearless

FEARLESS TAKEAWAY

Sometimes we are the solution.

FEARLESS NEXT STEPS

1. Those sacred spaces when we throw off the down comforter of safety for the downpour of sacrifice can become fertile ground for disappointment. The enemy wants us to believe that we seized a God-moment in vain when something doesn't turn out like we hoped it would. Where are you most vulnerable to believe "it's been useless?" Invite God to speak truth into those places.

2. James 3:17–18 defines wisdom this way: "But the wisdom that comes from heaven is first of all pure; then peace-loving, considerate, submissive, full of mercy and good fruit, impartial and sincere. Peacemakers who sow in peace reap a harvest of righteousness." With that as our standard, in what ways do you need God's help to walk in wisdom?

3. Wisdom walks us through these questions before we speak:

    Does it need to be said?
    When should it be said?
    How should it be said?

Consider writing these questions down or saving them in your phone for future conversations. As you use these criteria consistently, you'll develop a pattern that protects your relationships.

FEARLESS DECLARATION

I will not believe the lie that my prayers and integrity have been useless. I will let faith redirect my feelings to the truth of God's Word. I will filter my decisions through the lens of wisdom and bring peace into situations.

FEARLESS PRAYER

My prayer in my words...

Her Catalyst for Change—Stand Strong

As David and his army dined on a king-worthy culinary spread, Abigail led her convoy back home. Although her mission was a success, she braced for what she faced on the home-front. She knew her first order of business was to talk to her husband and explain the recent developments. We can only imagine the conversation she rehearsed in her head as she trekked back through the gulley. And we can only surmise her sentiments as she strode through the door.

"When Abigail went to Nabal, he was in the house holding a banquet like that of a king. He was in high spirits and very drunk. So she told him nothing at all until daybreak."

While David's men teetered on the brink of deprivation, and Abigail endangered her life, Nabal threw a party. *Ahem.* Abigail comes home to a staggering drunk, and she doesn't say a word. Wisdom doesn't just know what to say; it knows when to say nothing at all.

She understood the power of a well-timed word. I can't help but contemplate the many times I've spoken when I should've been silent. Our words have the power to shift the atmosphere and change the culture— for better or worse. Knowledge affords us the data we need to make an informed decision. But discernment grants us the good judgement we need to truly serve as a catalyst for change. No one grasped this better than another fearless heroine of the Bible, Queen Esther. Perhaps she gleaned from Abigail's example when she faced a dilemma of national proportions 500 years later.

Esther, an orphan raised by her religiously devoted cousin, Mordecai, was chosen by King Xerxes to replace Vashti, the deposed Queen of Persia. Her character and kindness won the favor of the people and the King himself. When Mordecai helped uncover a plot to kill Xerxes, he delivered the information to Esther, who warned him in the nick of time. However, when Mordecai, a Jew, refused to bow to the King's counselor, Haman, he became the target of Haman's evil design to murder all the Jews in the Persian Empire.

Haman made a persuasive, deception-laced case to the King, who agreed to genocide, unaware that his own Queen was a Jew. The threat of the Jews' imminent demise boosted Mordecai to counsel Esther and ask her to appeal to the King. She hesitated with good reason: to visit without invitation warranted death. Esther overcame fear to step into her calling. Esther 4:16 shares her response to Mordcai: "Go, gather together all the Jews who are in Susa, and fast for me. Do not eat or drink for three days, night or day. I and my attendants will fast as you do. When this is done, I will go to the king, even though it is against the law. And if I perish, I perish."

Her careful reply to the devastating news points to the depth of her character. It also reveals the reward of her pronouncement to pray and fast: God downloaded a plan. When Xerxes offered her anything she wanted, she strategically asked for a banquet in Haman's honor. She sat across the table from a man plotting to wipe out her entire race—not just one night, but two. She held her tongue because God held the power. On the eve of the second banquet, Esther spoke, and the truth of her words pierced the darkness. Haman was hung on the very gallows built for Mordecai, who took his role as counselor to the King. The Jews were saved, and Purim, a celebration of the event, became an official Jewish holiday.

Both women were fearless, putting themselves in danger to intervene for their lives and the lives of others. Both women weighed their words and exercised their influence. And both women stood strong as a catalyst for change. **We can hold our tongues when we trust that God holds the power.** The Holy Spirit guides us to distinguish when to put on the brakes, and when to gun it through the green light. Abigail and Esther portray the payoff when we let God determine our course of action when those around us make poor decisions. Let's head back over to the conclusion of our story in 1 Samuel 25:37.

"Then in the morning, when Nabal was sober, his wife told him all these things, and his heart failed him and he became like a stone. About ten days later, the Lord struck Nabal and he died."

Abigail tossed and turned throughout the night as her husband slept off his revelry. She was restless for the dawn of a new day so she could break the news to her husband. As she shared in vivid detail how he narrowly escaped death, he suffered what most believe was a massive stroke. Ten days later, Abigail was a widow.

"When David heard that Nabal was dead, he said, "Praise be to the Lord, who has upheld my cause against Nabal for treating me with contempt. He has kept his servant from doing wrong and has brought Nabal's wrongdoing down on his own head." Then David sent word to Abigail, asking her to become his wife. His servants went to Carmel and said to Abigail, "David has sent us to you to take you to become his wife." She bowed down with her face to the ground and said, "I am your servant and am ready to serve you and wash the feet of my lord's servants." Abigail quickly got on a donkey and, attended by her five female servants, went with David's messengers and became his wife."

She was God's divine provision in David's life, and he was hers. All the money in the world hadn't alleviated the heaviness in her home. Yet, humility guarded her from disobedience. Wisdom defended her from catastrophe. Silence safeguarded her from making a horrible situation worse. Not only did her actions prevent a shadow over her life, they helped David avoid one over his. And girls, she was right about David. In Acts 13, the apostle Paul spoke of God's feelings about King David: "After removing Saul, he made David their king. He testified concerning him: 'I have found David son of Jesse, a man after my own heart; he will do everything I want him to do.'"

She became the mother of Chileab and the loved wife of David. In 1 Samuel 30, we read how David returned the favor when he rescued her from abduction. If we're willing to look a little deeper into our story, we'll see a much broader picture. Nabal and David represent the two responses we give to the offer of salvation through God's Son. Nabal didn't repent, acknowledge his wrongdoing or thank Abigail for her intervention. David, on the other hand, responded tenderly, renouncing his intention for revenge. And our fearless Abigail beautifully depicted the mercy shown to us through Jesus Christ.

We, too, have the choice to reject or respond to God's mercy. We, too, have the choice to be an instrument of peace. When we're disappointed in life, let's not fall into the temptation of taking matters into our own hands. Let's not become enticed by the pull to self-help through revenge. Each time we seize an opportunity to inflict pain on someone who has caused us pain, we forfeit the opportunity to serve as a catalyst for change. Shame casts a long shadow. We can avoid unnecessary heartache when we listen to godly wisdom and seek the mind of God in a situation. We can stand strong with our dignity intact when we depend on His unfailing grace.

Find Your Fearless

FEARLESS TAKEAWAY

We can hold our tongues when we trust that God holds the power.

FEARLESS NEXT STEPS

1. Wisdom doesn't just know what to say; it knows when to say nothing at all. Abigail understood the power of a well-timed word. Take a moment to put yourself in Abigail's shoes when she returned home. When faced with disappointment and crushing circumstances, are you easily able to choose silence and exercise restraint? Why or why not?

2. Esther is praised for her fearless action to save her people. Yet, her decision was first bathed in prayer. "Go, gather together all the Jews who are in Susa, and fast for me. Do not eat or drink for three days, night or day. I and my attendants will fast as you do. When this is done, I will go to the king, even though it is against the law. And if I perish, I perish." What area of your life needs a divine strategy? Commit it to the Lord through prayer and fasting.

3. Humility guarded Abigail from disobedience. Wisdom defended her from catastrophe. Silence safeguarded her from making a horrible situation worse. Which of these areas necessitate the most attention in this season of your life?

FEARLESS DECLARATION

I will let humility guard me from disobedience. I will allow wisdom to defend my decisions. When silence is warranted, I will hold my tongue because I know God holds the power. I will trust Him to provide for every area of my life and stand strong through Him.

FEARLESS PRAYER

My prayer in my words…

Her Calling and Ours

If we took a moment to scroll Abigail's Instagram feed, we might find ourselves drooling over her latest recipe or clamoring for her beauty secrets. Then we'd listen to her recent podcast as she shares tips to keep your head about you while you're running a large-scale enterprise. She was drop-dead gorgeous, resourceful, and brilliant, but those weren't her strongest qualities. She weathered disappointment and dismantled conflict because she was wise.

Abigail knew when to act with urgency and when to wait. She led with humility and lived in a way that garnered the respect of others. She framed important information with discernment and seized critical moments because she knew the mind of God. In Abigail, we find so much more than a pretty face and a savvy manager. We find a brave woman who rose above bitter circumstances to bring peace when it was needed most. We discover the power of mercy to neutralize shrapnel. And we find our fearless in her story.

Maybe you're craving the courage to let your voice be heard in a loud world. Or you missed the memo that silence is golden, and you're bruised from backlash. Perhaps you're in a duel with depression from living with a difficult person. These are the moments that threaten to take us out. But they're also the very moments that test us so God can transform us. When we question if we're really cut out for this, God calls us to truly depend on Him.

We are not defined by the poor choices of those around us. Nor are we powerless when others with power act irresponsibly. Our words are often the impetus for action. Just look at how a handful of words altered the course of history.

"I have a dream." —Martin Luther King, Jr.

"Ask not what your country can do for you; ask what you can do for your country." —President John F. Kennedy, Jr.

"Do one thing every day that scares you." —Eleanor Roosevelt

"I have not failed. I have just found 10,000 ways that won't work."
—Thomas Edison

"No." —Rosa Parks

"It is finished." —Jesus

What about you? What if grace crafted your next sentence? What if prayer paved the way for your next decision? What if we stopped listening to fear and started listening for the voice of the Holy Spirit? God is looking for women who will stop succumbing to apathy and start walking in their calling. He uses women willing to ride into the heat of battle because they know His heart.

SEEK WISDOM

"The fear of the Lord is the beginning of wisdom; all who follow his precepts have good understanding." (Psalm 111:10)

Abigail was fearless because she was operating in wisdom. Her response to injustice was to do what was necessary to make it right. We can maintain our character no matter what is going on around us. Fearless women wrap every decision in wisdom. Heartache follows bad choices, especially when they go against the Word of God. Scripture contains guiding principles—not to limit our freedom—but to protect it. This applies to every area of our lives, especially marriage. Wisdom prepares us for the obvious and the unknown.

Wisdom waves a red flag when words like "maybe he'll change" or "maybe I can change him," come out of our mouths. Give your marriage a fighting chance by starting on the same page. God's design is not for a man and a woman to compete with one another, but to complete one another. The strongest foundation for marriage involves a husband and wife individually committed to Christ.

Wisdom warns us when we feel unnoticed, unappreciated, or unloved. Even the healthiest of marriages become sick through selfishness or sin. Pursue counsel at the first sign of danger. Don't wait until the cancer of unmet expectations has eaten away at your relationship. And beautiful girl, if your marriage failed, *you* are not a failure: you are dearly loved by God. He offers the grace we need to forgive ourselves when we've taken a wrong turn and to forgive others who've taken from us.

Wisdom protects us from exacting revenge when we've been treated unjustly. We can trust the character of God in all situations to defend us, protect us, and provide for us. Girls, wisdom is one of the most important pieces in your spiritual wardrobe. And it's highly versatile. It will keep you from overspending and underestimating. It will help you make the most of your time and make less of that offense. You can wear it at home, wear it to work, and wear it to ride a donkey into battle.

SEEK PEACE

"You will keep in perfect peace those whose minds are steadfast, because they trust in you." (Isaiah 26:3)

Wisdom prepares; peace repairs. Peace is a supernatural gift that comes from God, equipping us to rise above the raw emotions of a situation. We can keep our head about us in adversity when we let God keep us in perfect peace. God uses peace as a tool to repair the gaps brought on by anxiety and confusion. When we fix our eyes on Jesus, we find the peace we need to shift our perspective. Sometimes God changes our circumstances, and sometimes God changes us. Either one requires us to surrender completely to His purposes in and through us.

Peace seeks unity. Abigail sought to bring unity by mediating a conflict. She rose above her own frustration to ask David to rise above his. What is it you need to rise above? It's not worth derailing your destiny to retaliate when you could release. It's beneath you to gossip when you could let it go unsaid. We won't experience the meaningful relationships we long for or see growth in areas of our lives unless we're committed to resolving conflict. Matthew 18 coaches us in conflict resolution:

Try to resolve it one on one first. Listen for understanding and extend grace.

If that doesn't work, ask someone to come with you for the purpose of repairing what is broken.

If they're still unwilling to listen, let it go. Scripture instructs us to live in peace with one another, as far as it depends on you. When something is outside of your control, give it over to God.

SEEK OPPORTUNITIES

Fearless women wear wisdom, practice peace, and seek opportunities. Be on the lookout for doors of opportunity marked with God's fingerprints. Abigail tossed her apron and pulled on her riding boots. At great risk to herself, she put herself at the mercy of an angry man bent on revenge to intercede for her "bad boy" husband. And God changed the course of her destiny because of her obedience.

I can't help but wonder if Abigail's pillow was stained from tear-filled prayers asking God for divine opportunities. But when the moment came, I doubt very highly it looked anything like she had envisioned.

Our God-moments rarely do.

Abigail and Esther were both presented with the quandary to act in life and death situations. Each had to sit with the reality that something could go horribly wrong. They had to come to grips with the potential price of their choices. This is the plight of many missionaries around the world today who considered the cost and still said yes. Where does your heart beat alongside the heart of God for your culture? What would you risk your life for? Every choice, to act in faith or cower in fear, has a cost. Ask yourself these questions before you say yes to that opportunity:

Have I spent time in prayer listening for the God assignments?
Is this a battle God is calling me to fight?
Am I prepared through wisdom to act if the door opens?
How can I speak peace to repair a torn relationship?

Faith comes by hearing the Word of God. Are our ears open, girls? It just might be the sound of opportunity knocking. And when it does, we'll walk in humility and wisdom to step into our calling. We'll keep our wits about us while we manage a crisis. We'll handle conflict with grace because we've prayed that thing through. And girls, we'll seize the moment because we've sought the mind of God.

Find Your Fearless

FEARLESS TAKEAWAY

Wisdom prepares; peace repairs.

FEARLESS NEXT STEPS

1. Wisdom prepares us for the obvious and the unknown. Are you prepared through wisdom to act if a divine door of opportunity opens for you? Why or why not?

2. We can keep our head about us in adversity when we let God keep us in perfect peace. God uses peace as a tool to repair the gaps brought on by anxiety and confusion. Where do you need God to speak peace over your life? Where do you need to speak peace to repair something that is torn?

3. Identify where your heart beats alongside the heart of God for your culture. What would you risk your life for?

FEARLESS DECLARATION

I will spend time in prayer listening for my God assignments. I will look for His fingerprints on doors of opportunity and prepare myself through wisdom to move if the door opens. I will use my voice and speak peace to repair torn situations.

FEARLESS PRAYER

My prayer in my words...

The Samaritan Woman at the Well

Her Story & Our Starting Place

> When we refuse to cower to the voice of comparison, we change our culture.

JOHN 4

Before you begin your study, view the companion video resource here:

 www.angeladonadio.com

I have also included the video message and our key Scripture passage below.

\\|/

I trust you're seeing these women as more than just mere words on a page, but as real women you could talk to about real issues. Don't you wish you could pick Jochebed's brain for parenting advice? Or ask Abigail for strategies to effectively manage an organization? Rahab could most certainly help us yank off the rearview mirror of our past.

We're moving into the New Testament where we'll meet three more ordinary—but unforgettable—women. Long after David served as King, Israel split into the northern and southern kingdoms. In 722 BC, the northern kingdom fell to the Assyrians, who deported the Jews and repopulated the area with foreigners. The capital city of the northern kingdom at the time was Samaria. Some Jews remained, and others eventually returned and resettled, intermarrying with other cultures. This resulted in a mixed race of people, known eventually as "Samaritans." At the time of Jesus' ministry throughout the area, the Samaritans were despised by the Jews, for many reasons that we'll learn more about together. So much so, that the Jews avoided the major road, the trade route that ran through Samaria and crossed on the *other* side of the Jordan so they wouldn't have to have any involvement with them. Wow...talk about deep-seeded prejudice.

But as Jesus traveled from the Judean Desert north to Galilee, He didn't go around them. He traveled straight through a war zone to find one woman. We don't even know her name, but her unexpected encounter with Jesus altered the future of her entire community. At Jacob's well in this hated, forgotten place, Jesus had His longest recorded conversation in Scripture. To the Gospels we go!

 ## Live From The Mount Of Beatitudes

Girls, I'm at the Mount of Beatitudes, and behind me is the Sea of Galilee. It's actually a lake, and Jesus crossed its waters many times, most often by boat. *But*, there was that one time He walked on the water. A lot of His ministry took place in this region, and it was on one of His journeys here that He met a woman at a well in Samaria. Unlike Galilee, water was scarce in Samaria, and women travelled a good distance to draw water from a well. About noon that particular day, He engaged a broken woman in conversation—to fulfill her thirst, undo her shame, and bring the Gospel to all.

Let's read her story in John 4.

> "Now Jesus learned that the Pharisees had heard that he was gaining and baptizing more disciples than John— although in fact it was not Jesus who baptized, but his disciples. So he left Judea and went back once more to Galilee. Now he had to go through Samaria. So he came to a town in Samaria called Sychar, near the plot of ground Jacob had given to his son Joseph. Jacob's well was there, and Jesus, tired as he was from the journey, sat down by the well. It was about noon.

> When a Samaritan woman came to draw water, Jesus said to her, "Will you give me a drink?" (His disciples had gone into the town to buy food.) The Samaritan woman said to him, "You are a Jew and I am a Samaritan woman. How can you ask me for a drink?" (For Jews do not associate with Samaritans.) Jesus answered her, "If you knew the gift of God and who it is that asks you for a drink, you would have asked him and he would have given you living water."

> "Sir," the woman said, "you have nothing to draw with and the well is deep. Where can you get this living water? Are you greater than our father Jacob, who gave us the well and drank from it himself, as did also his sons and his livestock?"

Jesus answered, "Everyone who drinks this water will be thirsty again, but whoever drinks the water I give them will never thirst. Indeed, the water I give them will become in them a spring of water welling up to eternal life."

The woman said to him, "Sir, give me this water so that I won't get thirsty and have to keep coming here to draw water."

He told her, "Go, call your husband and come back."

"I have no husband," she replied.

Jesus said to her, "You are right when you say you have no husband. The fact is, you have had five husbands, and the man you now have is not your husband. What you have just said is quite true."

"Sir," the woman said, "I can see that you are a prophet. Our ancestors worshiped on this mountain, but you Jews claim that the place where we must worship is in Jerusalem."

"Woman," Jesus replied, "believe me, a time is coming when you will worship the Father neither on this mountain nor in Jerusalem. You Samaritans worship what you do not know; we worship what we do know, for salvation is from the Jews. Yet a time is coming and has now come when the true worshipers will worship the Father in the Spirit and in truth, for they are the kind of worshipers the Father seeks. God is spirit, and his worshipers must worship in the Spirit and in truth."

The woman said, "I know that Messiah" (called Christ) "is coming. When he comes, he will explain everything to us."

Then Jesus declared, "I, the one speaking to you—I am he."

Just then his disciples returned and were surprised to find him talking with a woman. But no one asked, "What do you want?" or "Why are you talking with her?"

Then, leaving her water jar, the woman went back to the town and said to the people, "Come, see a man who told me everything I ever did. Could this be the Messiah?" They came out of the town and made their way toward him.

Meanwhile his disciples urged him, "Rabbi, eat something." But he said to them, "I have food to eat that you know nothing about."

Then his disciples said to each other, "Could someone have brought him food?"

"My food," said Jesus, "is to do the will of him who sent me and to finish his work. Don't you have a saying, 'It's still four months until harvest'? I tell you, open your eyes and look at the fields! They are ripe for harvest. Even now the one who reaps draws a wage and harvests a crop for eternal life, so that the sower and the reaper may be glad together. Thus the saying 'One sows and another reaps' is true. I sent you to reap what you have not worked for. Others have done the hard work, and you have reaped the benefits of their labor."

Many of the Samaritans from that town believed in him because of the woman's testimony, "He told me everything I ever did." So when the Samaritans came to him, they urged him to stay with them, and he stayed two days. And because of his words many more became believers.

They said to the woman, "We no longer believe just because of what you said; now we have heard for ourselves, and we know that this man really is the Savior of the world.'"

Jesus exposed her sin—not to shame her—but to free her! For the first time in her life, she heard this message: You. Are. Not. Less. She looked in His eyes and no longer felt worthless or unloved. She felt significant and valued.

"This man…He sees the worst of me, and He still wants me."

I can only imagine her dusty feet that slowly plodded to the well that day now ran—with purpose—to get her entire community to come and meet this man named Jesus. She refused to cower to the voice of comparison she had listened to all her life and embraced her calling to change a culture.

◇◇◇

Each of my visits to Israel offered their own unique itinerary. However, one thing remains constant: *lots* of walking. Two thousand years ago, no one enjoyed the luxury of climbing into an air-conditioned bus. Travel was exhausting. With tired legs and a parched throat, Jesus sat to rest and drink. He knew that Jews believed they would become ceremonially unclean if they shared the drinking vessel of a Samaritan. But that didn't stop Him. Jesus never allowed man-made barriers to keep Him from divine appointments. He knew no one was exempt from grace. He invited her to leave the life she knew and find her identity in Him.

Jesus invites us to leave behind the fear that alienates others and extend the grace that includes. He invites us to stop the cycle of comparison and center our identity in Him. And we can say *yes*. We can follow her lead and invite Jesus to stay.

When we refuse to cower to the voice of comparison, we CHANGE OUR CULTURE.

Her Cause—Stand Up

The village stirred with the activity of morning routines. A month of abundant rainfall meant a full day for those harvesting barley and grapes. The market bustled with preparations to welcome harried travelers making their way through town. She peered out of the window and thought better of heading to the well just yet. The last thing she wanted was to be drawn into a conversation when she just needed to draw water. She winced and folded her arms tightly across her body. Even the simplest of tasks seemed complicated now, just like everything else in her life.

The noonday sun brought relative anonymity. After all, no respectable woman made this long trek in the scorching heat. She let out an awkward laugh. *"I'd rather wilt from heat exhaustion than from one more word of criticism,"* she thought to herself. She bent low to tie her sandals and ran her fingers over a new callous. Her hands looked weathered far beyond her years. As she hoisted her water pitcher for the journey, she noticed that the pain between her shoulder blades was worse than last week. She was so tired of walking this road...in more ways than one.

She stepped onto the low wall of limestone rock that surrounded the well and tried to ignore the man resting nearby. But she had no more pulled the rope through the deeply-set furrows when He spoke.

"Will you give me a drink?"

She was just trying to make it through another day in Sychar. She hadn't gone looking for a cause; but a cause found her.

That seemingly ordinary moment became a turning point in history. The conversation that followed transformed a broken woman into the first female evangelist. We don't even know her name, but her boldness revolutionized an entire town. That is a remarkable turn of events considering she had a few key strikes against her. She was relegated to the bottom of the social system, steeped in sin, and a Samaritan. She was as hardened as the region she lived in, made bitter by centuries of turmoil. In order to understand the significance of their conversation, let's backtrack a bit through the Old Testament.

Scripture first introduces us to this notorious location in Genesis 12, when Abraham built an altar at Shechem. Jacob followed suit in Genesis 33, later constructing a well on the same site. And it's at Jacob's well that an unnamed woman found her fearless when she encountered Jesus.

Samaria was the capital city of the northern kingdom of Israel. It was a large, splendid city, housing the road that served as the major trade route through the area. Once it was captured, Israel fell to the Assyrians. Jews faced mass deportations, calculated terror, and concentrated oppression. Samaria eventually became infiltrated by pagan religions as Jews and other races intermarried. They followed the Torah, the teachings of Moses contained in the first five books of the Bible. However, their belief in the one God became contaminated through the introduction of worship to other gods. Witchcraft and child sacrifice found their place alongside their own, modified version of the Torah.

As the rift intensified over time, John 8:38 tells us that that the Jews came to view the inhabitants of this area as "the worst of the human race." They accused the Samaritans of an "apostate" or renegade form of Yahweh worship because of their limited scope and understanding of Scripture. Rather than educate them, they deemed them unworthy of receiving truth. Irreconcilable differences led the Jews to avoid the Samaritans instead of investing in them. Throughout history, Samaria served as a haven for Jewish criminals, outlaws, and refugees from justice. The Jews considered the Samaritans the lowest of the low, regarding them as the most hated of any race. With that important historical context, let's take another look at our story.

"Now he had to go through Samaria. So he came to a town in Samaria called Sychar, near the plot of ground Jacob had given to his son, Joseph. Jacob's well was there, and Jesus, tired as he was from the journey, sat down by the well. It was about noon."

After a period of teaching and ministering across Judea, Jesus traveled north to Cana. Although the shortest route to Galilee traversed through the heart of Samaria, it was rarely used by Jews. Jesus knew the area had a long, complicated history. He knew a typical village day started at six in the morning. Yet he chose to travel straight through a combat zone.

At noon.

In the heat of the day.

In an area where water was scarce.

Jesus didn't *"have"* to go through Samaria: He chose to. This was not the act of a malfunctioning GPS or the accidental left turn of a lost tourist. This was an intentional, divine set-up. We're not sure that Jesus ever sipped a single drop of water from that well. But He accomplished what He came to do.

"When a Samaritan woman came to draw water, Jesus said to her, "Will you give me a drink?""

Jesus reached for a doozy of a conversation starter. A loaded question launched His longest, most intense dialogue with anyone in Scripture. Aaaaaaand, she was a woman. A Hebrew man wouldn't talk with a woman in the street; not even his own family. That, alone, would have come under strong criticism. But with one simple question, Jesus wasn't just addressing the rampant sexism of the day; He was taking on racial bigotry.

Jews refused to handle or consume food or drink touched by a Samaritan. Rabbis taught that to eat or drink anything produced or held by a Samaritan would render a Jew unclean. We'll delve into this more in our next session, but for now, it's important to know that the Old Testament Law taught extensively on the system of clean and unclean. An unclean person had to avoid that which was holy and observe complex steps to return to a state of cleanness. Uncleanness placed a person in a "dangerous" condition under threat of divine retribution, even death.[14]

Comparison chokes conversation. She knew full well what it would mean to hand him a cup. Racism was nothing new to her. She was accustomed to being disregarded and degraded. She barely even noticed anymore when someone shunned her for her lifestyle. Her quick response gave voice to a lifetime of comparison:

"The Samaritan woman said to him, "You are a Jew and I am a Samaritan woman. How can you ask me for a drink?" (For Jews do not associate with Samaritans.)"

All she had to do was give him a drink. She could've lowered her eyes as she lowered the rope. She could've avoided eye contact and evaded conversation. But she was intrigued at His inquiry. She was stunned by His request. She had been pummeled by prejudice and decimated by a ruined reputation. And after so many years of sitting in the mud of marginalization, she stood up. She stood up to speak up. She refused to allow the crippling weight of comparison to keep her from conversation. She was so used to fighting for herself, she could scarcely comprehend the revelation that someone was fighting for her. For the first time in her life, *she* was the cause worth fighting for.

When Jesus came on the scene, He challenged every religious teaching of the day. He not only spoke well of the Samaritans, He healed one of leprosy and rebuked two disciples for wanting to destroy them with fire. He was above all racial prejudices and religious preferences. He knew that this woman, deemed by the world as a lost cause, was a source of untapped kingdom potential. And as she kicked fear to the literal curb, she met a man unlike any she had ever known.

Girls, fear draws a thick dividing line. We tend to avoid what we fear and sidestep what we don't understand. **We can choose another way: we can love like Jesus.** Jesus didn't just fight for her—He fights for us. He fights for every ounce of dormant potential He sees in us, so we'll step into our calling. He fights for every piece of our heart, so we'll know our worth. Because when we do, we find our fearless and fight for others. John, the beloved disciple of Jesus, wrote prolifically about the kind of love that drives out fear in 1st John 4. I don't think it's any surprise that he's the one that penned our story. He gets it, girls, and we can, too.

"There is no fear in love. But perfect love drives out fear, because fear has to do with punishment. The one who fears is not made perfect in love. We love because He first loved us."

Find Your Fearless

FEARLESS TAKEAWAY

We can choose another way: we can love like Jesus.

FEARLESS NEXT STEPS

1. After so many years of sitting in the mud of marginalization, she stood up. She stood up to speak up. She refused to allow the crippling weight of comparison to keep her from conversation. Jesus invites us to dialogue. What situations tend to silence your voice through comparison? Talk to Him about it and listen for His guidance.

2. John, the beloved disciple of Jesus, wrote prolifically about the kind of love that drives out fear in 1 John 4. In the NIV, John uses a form of the word, "love," 27 times in 14 verses. Take a moment to read verses 7–21 and write your thoughts here.

3. Fear draws a thick dividing line. We tend to avoid what we fear and sidestep what we don't understand. Have you found this to be true in your own life? If so, what's one way you can begin to love like Jesus?

FEARLESS DECLARATION

I will stop allowing comparison to keep me silent. I will ask God to help me see myself the way He sees me so I can truly know my worth in Him. I will never write anyone off as a lost cause. I will fight for the kingdom potential in others because Jesus fights for me.

FEARLESS PRAYER

My prayer in my words…

Her Choice—Stand Out

Search the Scriptures high and low, but you'll never find Jesus drawn into an argument. It certainly wasn't for lack of opportunity. Satan, the religious leaders, and His disciples—just to name a few—tried their best to pull Him toward disputes. He never shied away from dialogue, but He refused to engage in debate. He employed carefully placed questions, correction, and compassionate understanding to communicate with a variety of audiences. And with our woman of the hour, He masterfully utilized all three.

Their compelling conversation reveals an important truth about Jesus: He wasn't afraid of anything. Nothing was off limits because nothing mattered more than leading her to salvation...

Not her gender...so they talked. Period.

Not her ethnicity...so they talked about her race.

Not her social status...so they talked about her position in the community.

Not her secrets...so they talked about her lifestyle.

Not her questions...so they talked about history and theology.

Yet, while she attempted to focus on temporal things, Jesus continually shifted her attention to the eternal. As He revealed Himself, she stopped cowering to comparison and stepped into her calling. Although she came to draw water, He came to draw her to a new way of life.

Jesus answered her, "If you knew the gift of God and who it is that asks you for a drink, you would have asked him and he would have given you living water."

"Sir," the woman said, "you have nothing to draw with and the well is deep. Where can you get this living water? Are you greater than our father Jacob, who gave us the well and drank from it himself, as did also his sons and his livestock?"

Jesus answered, "Everyone who drinks this water will be thirsty again, but whoever drinks the water I give them will never thirst. Indeed, the water I give them will become in them a spring of water welling up to eternal life." The woman said to him, "Sir, give me this water so that I won't get thirsty and have to keep coming here to draw water.""

She linked together a series of phrases that were pregnant with one word: possibility. And possibility, girls, implies hope. Her spine straightened with courage. Her veins coursed with expectancy. Her mind probed with fresh promise.

> "How is it possible for this man to draw water? What does he have that our forefathers didn't have? What does he know that I don't know? And how do I get this water?"

This is the foundation of the Great Exchange. She offered a limited source of water and He offered an immeasurable and infinite supply. Yet, even as slivers of possibility streamed light into her dark places, she couldn't see the whole picture. She wanted Him to meet a pressing need, but He longed to meet her deepest need. His words weren't cryptic; they were crystal clear.

> *"Ask Me. I'll give you eternal life."*

In her limited understanding, she requested a lifetime supply of water. Before we shake our heads in disbelief, let's shed some honesty on our own decisions. Isn't that just like us, girls? We're quickly engulfed by the tyranny of the urgent or the quest for convenience. But Jesus didn't call us to a life of comfort; He called us to a life of purpose. Thankfully, He doesn't give up when we don't get it. He changes the direction of conversation to challenge our choices.

"He told her, "Go, call your husband and come back."

"I have no husband," she replied.

Jesus said to her, "You are right when you say you have no husband. The fact is, you have had five husbands, and the man you now have is not your husband. What you have just said is quite true."

"Sir," the woman said, "I can see that you are a prophet. Our ancestors worshiped on this mountain, but you Jews claim that the place where we must worship is in Jerusalem."

"Woman," Jesus replied, "believe me, a time is coming when you will worship the Father neither on this mountain nor in Jerusalem. You Samaritans worship what you do not know; we worship what we do know, for salvation is from the Jews. Yet a time is coming and has now come when the true worshipers will worship the Father in the Spirit and in truth, for they are the kind of worshipers the Father seeks. God is spirit, and his worshipers must worship in the Spirit and in truth.""

Well, okay then. Let's go there. Jews taught that a woman might be divorced twice and *at most* three times. As women couldn't divorce men, she wore the stigma of rejection and the scarlet letter of adultery. We don't know all the extenuating circumstances, but we know she was embarrassed by the depth of her sinful choices. She assumed she was in the presence of a prophet and became uncomfortable by his knowledge of her immoral lifestyle. As she tried to redirect Him to resolve an age-old dispute, He sought to reassure her that the most secret and sacred areas of her life were safe with Him.

He wanted her to understand that worship isn't a place; it's a posture of the heart. It's not a "where;" it's a "who." Religion is man's attempt to get to God. But Jesus is God's attempt to get to man. He wanted her to stop dwelling on religious rules and start developing a relationship with Him. She was a hot mess, and He didn't let her off the hot seat. He had to expose her sin and clean out the contamination of her heart before she could hold the gift of living water. His words weren't an indictment; they were an invitation.

> *"Stop. Stop comparing yourself to others and destroying your life. Stop believing that you're not worth more than this. You are. I know all of it...I do. But I can redeem it. And I'll use it in ways you never dreamed. You don't have to feel isolated and ignored one more minute; you just have to make a choice."*

Her sin laid bare, she calculated her next move. We'll pitch our tent on the edge of this cliff for a moment. As we examine their conversation and analyze her choices, let's pause to take an inventory of our own. When's the last time you sat and had a gut-wrenchingly honest conversation with Jesus? And when we do, do we really listen for His heart? Can you sense what He's trying to say to you?

> *Yes, it's possible.*
> *Ask Me.*
> *Stop.*

We can only truly walk in our calling when we've heard His voice. We are the pitcher that carries His living water. We pour out our worship when it flows from a surrendered heart. We impact those around us when we let Jesus guide our conversations. Girls, sometimes it's so much easier to put up an argument than to put out a hand. Fear alienates, but faith engages. It's not our responsibility to convict people of sin; that's the Holy Spirit's role. He does His best work when we let Him do His job. When you invite someone to experience relationship rather than religion, the conversation shifts.

The world doesn't need one more debate; it needs Jesus. It needs fearless women who will stand out for the way they treat others. It needs compassionate women who talk *to* people instead of *at* them. It needs empathetic women who listen for someone's pain point and remind them that they matter. It needs women who point people to Jesus so He can quench their thirst. Who's waiting at the well for you? You don't need a water jar to seize your next God-moment. Just open your eyes and you'll discover a world of possibilities.

Find Your Fearless

FEARLESS TAKEAWAY

Worship isn't a place; it's a posture of the heart.

FEARLESS NEXT STEPS

1. We're quickly engulfed by the tyranny of the urgent or the quest for convenience. But Jesus didn't call us to a life of comfort; He called us to a life of purpose. Where is He challenging your choices?

2. When's the last time you sat and had a gut-wrenchingly honest conversation with Jesus? What do you sense Him trying to say to you in this season?

3. It's not our responsibility to convict people of sin; that's the Holy Spirit's role. He does His best work when we let Him do His job. Is this hard for you? Why or why not?

FEARLESS DECLARATION

I will allow the Holy Spirit full access to the secret and sacred areas of my life. I will make conversation with Jesus my top priority and truly listen for His heart. I will be a woman who talks to others and not at them. I will point people to Jesus so He can quench their thirst.

FEARLESS PRAYER

My prayer in my words...

Her Catalyst for Change—Stand Strong

What happens when uncommon faith has an unexpected encounter with an extraordinary God? It looks something like John, Chapter 4. We last left our heroine-to-be in a predicament. A chance meeting at a well caught her by surprise. Countless attempts to satisfy the thirst of her soul had only left her dangerously dehydrated. She desperately wanted to believe that her search for significance was over.

"How does he know these things about me? Dare I trust him? Or will this turn out to be just another huge disappointment? Why should I expect to be treated any differently than other women like me?"

She was aware of the punishment laid out in the Old Testament Law for a woman in a similar condition. Tucked away in the 5th Chapter of Numbers was the "trial by ordeal." It was a process outlined in the Law as a means of revealing potentially hidden sin. This "test for an unfaithful wife" demanded an accused woman to, in Matthew Henry's words, "stand as a spectacle to the world."[15]

If a wife's character and honesty came in question by a jealous or suspicious husband, the investigation first required a grain offering to draw attention to guilt and shame. Barnes tells us the husband was required to bring the priest the cheapest and coarsest kind of barley, representing the abused condition of the suspected woman.[16]

To show the gravity of the situation and cause her to feel the condemnation of sin, it was compulsory that she stand in public while the priest took dust from the tabernacle floor. He put it into holy water in a ceremonially clean vessel consecrated for the humiliating ritual he was about to perform. He loosened her hair as a sign of guilt and uncovered her head as a token of her shame. As she held the barley, a reminder of sin, the priest held the bitter water and put her under oath. He read aloud a curse of unimaginable proportions for a woman in the ancient Near East: the loss of the capacity to bear a child. He wrote the curses on a scroll, blotted them out with a wet sponge, washed them off into the water, and made her drink the cup. If she was lying about her infidelity, the curse would cause her abdomen to swell, indicating guilt. If not, she was exonerated.

The prophet Isaiah announced the dawn of a new morning: "I, even I, am he who blots out your transgressions, for my own sake, and remembers your sins no more. But he was pierced for our transgressions, he was crushed for our iniquities; the punishment that brought us peace was on him, and by his wounds we are healed. We all, like sheep, have gone astray, each of us has turned to our own way, and the Lord has laid on him the iniquity of us all." Isaiah 43:25, 53:5–6.

God placed the curse of sin on Jesus at Calvary. The Jews turned Him over to the Romans who tore out His beard, flogged Him in public, and hung Him naked on a cross. He stood as a spectacle to the world to remove our shame and reconcile us back to God. At His final meal with the disciples, the Lord's Supper, He drank the cup of suffering as He told them what was to come. On the cross, knowing all that was completed, He uttered three words to fulfill Scripture: "I am thirsty." As the guards handed him a sponge formed from a hyssop plant and soaked in bitter wine-vinegar, He tasted death for our salvation and blotted away our iniquity. He came to lift us out of condemnation, take our pain, and fulfill our thirst.

Why did He walk that dusty road to Samaria? Because He would soon walk the Via Dolorosa to the cross. He asked her for a cup of water because He would soon drink our curse. He engaged her in conversation because He would soon fulfill the ceremonial law, giving us forgiveness of sins and eternal life with Him. Even with the Samaritans' incomplete knowledge of the first five books of the Old Testament, they anticipated the arrival of the Messiah along with the Jews. She just had no idea He was sitting right in front of her.

"The woman said, "I know that Messiah" (called Christ) "is coming. When he comes, he will explain everything to us." Then Jesus declared, "I, the one speaking to you—I am he.""

Those three words mark the first time Jesus openly revealed Himself as the Messiah. It wasn't livestreamed to every media outlet or lauded with a parade. It wasn't at a political rally or in a stadium surrounded by 70,000 screaming fans. It was in an intimate conversation with an unnamed woman on an ordinary day. But not just any woman. A woman who believed that the Messiah would come, and when He did, He would clear up all the confusion. He would make everything right. She had the faith to seize the moment and serve as a catalyst for change. As the disciples returned from purchasing food, I'm not sure if they were more shocked to see Jesus talking to a woman, or to watch her dashing back to town.

"Then, leaving her water jar, the woman went back to the town and said to the people, 'Come, see a man who told me everything I ever did. Could this be the Messiah?' They came out of the town and made their way toward him."

Girls, close your eyes and imagine this scene for just a moment. Men…women…children…all streaming toward Jesus. And they're led by a woman who dared to believe it was possible. All the critics were silenced. All the arguments were gone. While the crowd made its way to Jesus, He made a point to His disciples.

> *"Don't you have a saying that it's still four months until harvest? Look. See all those people coming this way? The harvest is here. This town, full of the people you didn't think deserved the good news, will hear it straight from Me. They're ready for My message. This is what I came to do."*

Although the disciples missed the opportunity to seize this moment, she didn't. She commanded everyone's attention and introduced them to Christ. Because she bravely shared her story, an entire town met Jesus.

"Many of the Samaritans from that town believed in him because of the woman's testimony, 'He told me everything I ever did.' So when the Samaritans came to him, they urged him to stay with them, and he stayed two days. And because of his words many more became believers. They said to the woman, "We no longer believe just because of what you said; now we have heard for ourselves, and we know that this man really is the Savior of the world."

She didn't just leave her water jar at the well that day. She let go of the sin that held her captive and the cycle of comparison that held her back. She could've weaponized that moment in retaliation against those that had hurt her and kept it to herself. But the instant she realized Jesus was the Messiah, and experienced the truth of His love, she didn't think twice about sharing it with others. Her entire community urged Him to stay with them for two days. We too can say "yes" to Jesus. We can follow her lead and invite Jesus to stay.

She stood strong as a powerful witness and the first female evangelist recorded in the New Testament. The book of Acts continues what she started. Four years later, Philip, the evangelist, walked through the door she opened to bring salvation to many in the region.

"Those who had been scattered preached the word wherever they went. Philip went down to a city in Samaria and proclaimed the Messiah there. When the crowds heard Philip and saw the signs he performed, they all paid close attention to what he said. For with shrieks, impure spirits came out of many, and many who were paralyzed or lame were healed. So there was great joy in that city."

Acts 8 shares that the disciples called Peter and John to come to Samaria and pray for those who believed on Jesus to receive the Holy Spirit. The fearless woman who dared to start a conversation started a revival.

Who needs to hear your story? If you've had an encounter with Christ, bring someone else along with you. Don't get derailed by meaningless arguments: stick to your story. Tell people how Jesus changed your life and become a catalyst for change in theirs. Everyone is thirsty. We carry an insatiable yearning for the eternal because we were created in the image of God. Everyone deserves the opportunity to hear Jesus say those same, life-changing words He said to her: You. Are. Not. Less. Remember who you were before you met Christ and the situations that made you feel "less-than." Then let that light a fire under you for the lost. ***Look. See all those people coming this way? The harvest is here.***

Find Your Fearless

FEARLESS TAKEAWAY

Jesus, stay.

FEARLESS NEXT STEPS

1. She could've weaponized the moment she met Jesus in retaliation against those that had hurt her and kept it to herself. But the instant she realized Jesus was the Messiah, and experienced the truth of His love, she didn't think twice about sharing it with others. Who needs to hear your story? Don't keep it to yourself.

2. The prophet Isaiah announced the dawn of a new morning: "Surely He has borne our iniquities. The punishment for our sin was laid on Him." Take a moment to read Isaiah 43 and 53 and thank Jesus for what He has done for you.

3. Remember who you were before you met Christ and those situations that made you feel "less-than." If they still hold any power over you, ask the Holy Spirit for the grace to forgive and let go. Then, let that light a fire under you for the lost.

FEARLESS DECLARATION

I am not less. I am bought with the precious blood of Jesus and loved unconditionally. I will open my eyes to see the harvest in front of me and share my story with others. I will dare to dream for revival in my community and let it start with me.

FEARLESS PRAYER

My prayer in my words…

Her Calling and Ours

"Chasha." "Tovah." "Yael."

I resisted the temptation to give our girl a name. I mean, any one of those sounds so much nicer than "unnamed woman." But that's part of the point. "The Samaritan woman" says everything we need to know. She's any one of us who has ever felt less than or left out. Marginalized or mocked. Discriminated against or deemed unworthy. Eleanor Roosevelt uttered some of my favorite words of all time, including these: "No one can make you feel inferior without your consent."[17] Although that's entirely true, it's not entirely easy to do.

Raw emotions can hijack our best intentions and build barriers to fearless living. Perhaps you've found yourself feeling…

Less than while you're sitting in a waiting room for another infertility appointment.

Left out when no one notices you're gone.

Marginalized when your paycheck is not as much as your male co-worker's.

Mocked as you take a pro-life stance.

Discriminated against for the color of your skin.

Deemed unworthy because of the address on your driver's license.

Jesus never allowed man-made barriers to keep Him from divine appointments. When we refuse to cower to the voice of comparison, we change a culture. When we stop feeling ashamed for things we can't control, we stand up and speak up. When we're not afraid to stand out for our faith, we give the Holy Spirit room to move. When we leave our water jar at the well, we find ourselves in amazing company. Fearless women overcome obstacles posed by gender, race, or socio-economic status, to step into their calling.

Let's go out of our way to reach people instead of going around them. When we stop avoiding what we don't understand and start building relationships, we'll bring people to Christ. It all begins with a conversation.

START A CONVERSATION

We won't know what to say to others unless we've first talked to Jesus. The Samaritan woman stopped listening to the narrative of the world and started listening to Jesus' voice. We settle our sideways emotions in Jesus' presence. His Word renews our faulty thought patterns and replaces them with Truth. **We'll be the best version of ourselves in public when we've spent time with Jesus in private.** We don't have to wait until we've gotten it all together. Girls, none of us do. Bring that messy bun and even messier situation. He wants to know everything. *All. The. Things.* Talk it out so it doesn't take you out. He'll change us in His presence so we can become a catalyst for change in our world.

Nothing replaces a face-to-face encounter. Jesus didn't write a text or sling judgement through a computer screen. He didn't glance at his overscheduled calendar and send someone else in His place. He sat in the dirt with one person who needed His full attention. He dropped everything to stay.

What about us? Are we trying to win an argument or win someone to Christ? We love like Jesus when we start a conversation instead of a debate. We love like Jesus when we want to do right more than we want to be right. Our personal war-zones may not look like a town in the heart of the Middle East. But they might look like our social media channels… and our offices… and our homes. Let's bring Jesus into the conversation and invite Him to stay.

STOP THE MADNESS

We learn the math symbols for *"greater than and lesser than"* early in our elementary school years. However, we carry the concept throughout our adult lives by one word: comparison. Inherent in the concept of comparison is the idea that someone is better than someone else. It manifests itself in two ways: insecurity and inequality.

INSECURITY

Someone will always be something *"-er"* more than you or me. It's lethal to fix our eyes on something we lack and focus where we feel someone else has it in spades. When we look at the lives of others through the blurred lens of jealousy or resentment, we get stuck in the vicious cycle of comparison. When our life isn't turning out the way we thought it should, or someone else's seems so much more "er" than ours, insecurity whispers the lie that God isn't good. Or if He is, He just isn't good to us. The enemy loves nothing more than to get us to question God's character. When we do, we express discontent with His will. We can choose to trust God's character even when we don't understand our circumstances. We can choose contentment even when we're confused. We can choose gratitude even when we're disappointed. Girls, we'll develop the God-confidence we need to combat insecurity when we ground our identity in Christ.

INEQUALITY

We can applaud our heroine from a distance, but the real test comes in how we treat people. Her passion for the lost moved me to do some serious soul-searching. Discrimination of any kind has no place in the body of Christ. The story in John, Chapter 4 could just have easily been written in last month's paper. It contains critical insight for the complex dilemmas we face today.

First, Jesus demolished centuries of dogma driven by hatred. When we allow preconceived ideas to create personal bias, we alienate people from the Gospel. It's this same book of John that contains one of the most recognizable verses of Scripture: "For God so loved the world, that He gave His only begotten Son; that whosoever believeth in Him should not perish, but have everlasting life," John 3:16. Who is our "whosoever?" Who do we tend to keep at arm's length from the Gospel? A terrorist? A sex-offender? Someone who doesn't think like me?

Second, we don't have to agree with someone to honor them. I had the opportunity to interview Caleb Kaltenbach, Author of *"Messy Grace: How a Pastor with Gay Parents Learned to Love Others Without Sacrificing Conviction."* As he shared his compelling story, I was profoundly impacted by this statement: "Acceptance is not agreement."[18] Jesus didn't avoid the necessary discussion of sin, and neither should we. But we filter conversations through the love of Jesus. Condemnation separates but conviction softens.

Girls, let's stop the madness. Don't feed insecurity or foster inequality. Instead, let's ground ourselves in the Word so we know our worth. Let's get out of our comfort zones so we can step into our calling. Let's bring people to Jesus so He can change their lives.

SHARE YOUR STORY

Never underestimate the power of one. The Samaritan woman made the most of her unexpected encounter with Jesus. She immediately left what was familiar to step far outside her comfort zone. Her story became the bridge that enabled an entire town to cross over to Jesus.

Once we encounter Jesus, we are never the same. Ordinary moments become divine opportunities to share our story. The enemy wants us to believe the lie that something disqualifies us from telling others about Jesus. He disparages us for our lack of knowledge of Scripture or belittles us because of our past. He wants us to remain isolated and ineffective. The Samaritan woman didn't have a pristine reputation or master's degree in theology. What she did have, however, was a story.

"You have to come with me. I just met Jesus, the Messiah! He's here at the well! Hurry! Get your family and follow me. I can't even describe it. He knew everything about me and still offered to give me eternal life. All I had to do was ask Him. I can't wait for you to meet Him, too."

What does your invitation sound like? Simply share Jesus. Your story may be the bridge that brings someone else to freedom.

Find Your Fearless

FEARLESS TAKEAWAY

We'll be the best version of ourselves in public when we've spent time with Jesus in private.

FEARLESS NEXT STEPS

1. We settle our sideways emotions in Jesus' presence. Identify any emotional barriers to fearless living. Talk it out so it doesn't take you out.

2. John 3:16 shares, "For God so loved the world, that He gave His only begotten Son; that whosoever believeth in Him should not perish but have everlasting life." Who is your "whosoever?" Who do you tend to keep at arm's length from the Gospel? Ask Jesus to forgive any places of personal prejudice and help you to love people the way He does.

3. The Samaritan woman didn't have a pristine reputation or a master's degree in theology. What she did have, however, was a story. What does your invitation sound like?

FEARLESS DECLARATION

I will trade my "less-than" raw emotions for the truth of God's Word. I will do my part to stop the madness. I refuse to feed insecurity or foster inequality. I will be the bridge that brings someone to Jesus.

FEARLESS PRAYER

My prayer in my words…

The Woman with the Issue of Blood

Her Story & Our Starting Place

> A moment in God's presence
> can remedy a lifetime of pain.

MARK 5:21—34

Before you begin your study, view the companion video resource here:

www.angeladonadio.com

I have also included the video message and our key Scripture passage below.

Welcome back! Aren't these women amazing? Each one impacted their families, changed cultures, and influenced future generations. No one validated the worth of women more than Jesus. He spent three years in public ministry traveling through various regions to fulfill His earthly mission. On more than one occasion, He shocked the religious leaders of the day by placing more value on people than He did on protocol. Much to their chagrin, He healed on the Sabbath, played with children, and ate with sinners. He returned to the area of Galilee many times, and on one occasion, Luke's Gospel tells us that the crowds were so great they nearly crushed Jesus. A woman heard He was in town—a woman desperate for a miracle. She suffered for 12 years from an incurable illness that stole her health, her finances, and her identity. Levitical Law considered her "ceremonially unclean." Treated as an outcast, she was prevented from worshiping in the temple, forced into a life of loneliness, and barred from physical touch. *For 12 years.*

She pushed through humiliation and hardship to get to Jesus. But Jesus wasn't daunted by her infirmity. She didn't make Him unclean; He made her whole.

Live From Capernaum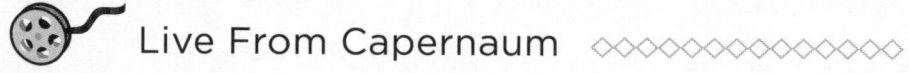

I'm in Capernaum, the base of Jesus' early ministry, the home of Peter, and the site of many healings. This is where Jesus encountered the woman with the issue of blood. She had been hurting for so long, she didn't even remember what it felt like to be normal anymore. Jesus was swarmed by crowds, and He was on an urgent mission to get to the house of a religious leader named Jairus, whose 12-year-old daughter was dying. But none of that kept Jesus from stopping. Their story is recorded in Matthew, Mark and Luke's Gospels, and we'll read Mark's account.

Mark Chapter 5:21–34

"When Jesus had again crossed over by boat to the other side of the lake, a large crowd gathered around him while he was by the lake. Then one of the synagogue leaders, named Jairus, came, and when he saw Jesus, he fell at his feet. He pleaded earnestly with him, "My little daughter is dying. Please come and put your hands on her so that she will be healed and live."" So Jesus went with him.

A large crowd followed and pressed around him. And a woman was there who had been subject to bleeding for twelve years. She had suffered a great deal under the care of many doctors and had spent all she had, yet instead of getting better she grew worse. When she heard about Jesus, she came up behind him in the crowd and touched his cloak, because she thought, "If I just touch his clothes, I will be healed." Immediately her bleeding stopped and she felt in her body that she was freed from her suffering.

At once Jesus realized that power had gone out from him. He turned around in the crowd and asked, "Who touched my clothes?"

"You see the people crowding against you," his disciples answered, "and yet you can ask, 'Who touched me?'"

But Jesus kept looking around to see who had done it. Then the woman, knowing what had happened to her, came and fell at his feet and, trembling with fear, told him the whole truth. He said to her, "Daughter, your faith has healed you. Go in peace and be freed from your suffering.""

I'm so moved by the fearless faith of this anonymous woman. She was weak and worn-down. She wanted to hide at the back and disappear into the crowd. She was terrified of being rebuked by this Rabbi, Jesus, or turned away. Yet, she summoned the courage to move forward in confidence. She knew that if she could just touch Jesus, she would never be the same. See, we can try and hide our private pain, for whatever reason, but Jesus knows—and Jesus cares. He honored the faith of this ordinary woman that propelled her to overcome barriers and dare to do extraordinary things.

◇◇◇

I'm holding an authentic tallit, given to me by a team member on our trip to Israel. This unique garment, usually made of wool or linen, is the type of prayer shawl worn by Jesus. The fringed tassels bear special significance, described in the Old Testament as reminders of the commandments of God. The woman we're studying this week braved the crowd to touch the hem of his garment—the tallit. Yet, Jesus used the very symbol of the law as an opportunity to demonstrate grace. Her desperation became a platform for the miraculous.

As a survivor of two near-death experiences, I empathize with her plight and understand her pain. I wrote about my health challenges in my first book, *"Finding Joy When Life is Out of Focus: A Study of Philippians for Joy-Thirsty Women."* I endured an excruciating battle with endometriosis, replete with years of difficult medical treatments, and nearly died from a rare, life-threatening disorder. As we find our fearless in her story, allow me a moment to share some of mine in the excerpt below:

"In 2001, after living with chronic pain from endometriosis, I had a hysterectomy. One week after surgery, I was bleeding badly enough at home to call my doctor. After following his advice and going to the emergency room, they admitted me for observation. To make a long story short, over the course of twelve hours, while fully awake, I lost over half of my blood. Nurses frantically came in and out of my hospital room attempting to stop me from hemorrhaging to death. At 3:30 AM, I looked at the clock and terror became my bedside visitor. I thought to myself, "I'm not going to make it until 6:00 AM when my doctor is on call." That proved to be a defining moment in my life. God was refocusing my lens.

Later, as I was still processing all that had happened, I said to the Lord, "I don't ever want to feel that desperate again." I heard Him respond, "That is how I always want you to feel—that dependent on Me." God was changing the faulty thought patterns that threatened to choke out my joy. I "died" to self in that hospital in a tangible way. I began to journal during this period of my life and my relationship with the Lord became much more intimate and personal. My thoughts and questions became songs that eventually formed my first album, "This Journey."

In 2003, I began to feel ill and experience sharp pain I had never known before. I had no appetite and struggled for several months, losing weight and enduring bouts of excruciating pain. After weeks of doctor visits, I was admitted to the hospital. My heart rate had plummeted to 41 beats per minute and my blood pressure was hovering dangerously low at 76/40. I spent eleven days in the hospital with nothing to eat or drink until the doctors scheduled an extensive MRI.

Lying on my side in the only position my body could tolerate, completely alone, I watched the screen as the barium reached my stomach and stopped. The forty-five-minute GI test took seven hours. I lay on the cold, metal table hour after hour—drink, sit up, roll over, stand up, lay down, drink—and I heard the Lord say to me, "Angela, I know you can worship me in the sanctuary. I want to know if you can worship me here." I have led worship hundreds of times, but this hospital room became holy ground. I sang quietly with tears flowing down my face, "Here I am to worship. Here I am to bow down. Here I am to say that you're my God." That moment of surrender ushered in my miracle.

There are no coincidences in God. A doctor on call at the hospital saw my films and happened to be studying for his medical board exams. He remembered a picture that looked like my films. They called in more specialists and finally gave me a diagnosis at 7:00 AM the next morning— Superior Mesenteric Artery Syndrome. SMA Syndrome is a rare, life-threatening disorder where the superior mesentery artery takes too sharp a right turn. The first portion of my intestines, my duodenum, was compressing the artery and acting as an obstruction. A severely compressed artery kept my stomach from emptying properly. Two days later, a team of specialists made the decision to perform a duodenal jejunostomy to bypass the affected portion of my intestines and relieve pressure on the artery. Then, they would reconnect the stomach to a lower section of the intestines.

The day of surgery was my low point. We didn't know if I would make it. I remember asking God, "What else could I need to learn? Why is this happening to me?" God reassured that this did not take Him by surprise. I survived the surgery, and after one more difficult week in the hospital, I went home. I spent months reeling from trauma, adjusting to a scar than ran the length of my torso, and unable to eat solid food. Even in those dark days, God was whispering to me, breathing hope into my withered spirit. While recuperating, I took out a piece of paper and scribbled these words:

"I don't understand how this is in your plan, but I'll trust you anyhow. I can't possibly see what good is there for me, but I'll trust you anyhow." This song completed my first album. This became a new way of living for me; learning to trust God's character completely, even when life is out of focus."

Jesus isn't intimidated by our issues. He wants us to press through until His touch makes us whole. Let's unpack the powerful truth this woman already knew: A moment in God's presence can remedy a lifetime of pain.

A moment
IN GOD'S
PRESENCE can
remedy a lifetime
of pain.

Her Cause—Stand Up

Freshly laundered linen swayed in the cool, lake breeze. The excitement in her neighbors' voices stirred her from a deep sleep. She pushed up onto her elbows and let her legs dangle over the side of the bed. She felt foggy. Disoriented. She caught the basin of dirty water out of the corner of her eye and tried to remember how long it had been there. A day? Two? She couldn't seem to keep up with anything, anymore. Everything was just one giant blur. She had every intention of carrying the basin outside after she washed the blood from her clothes. But it was too heavy. She was too spent.

She picked up a small mirror, one of the few things she hadn't sold to pay for the treatments. Now, it was nothing more than a cruel reminder of her life before this wretched disease. The trademark flush of her cheeks and the fleck in her hazel eyes faded behind pale skin and dark circles. Afraid she might faint again, she braced herself and garnered the strength to stand.

She untied the thin string holding the small pouch. She didn't need to bother counting, but she couldn't help herself. Five shekels. *Five.* After twelve long years, only a few thin coins stood between her and death.

"Well, this is it, then," she said aloud to no one in particular. Bankrupt and broken, she glanced at the stone steps outside her front door. She knew Jesus was in town; the news was everywhere. Blind men received their sight and lame men walked. The crowds were massive. *"Hmmmm...the crowd,"* she thought to herself. *"Maybe I won't even be noticed. If I can just make it one more day. If I can just ..."*

In Matthew, Mark, and Luke's Gospels, we read the story of a woman decimated by disease. She braved weakness and the threat of disgrace to experience a powerful encounter with Jesus Christ. Although we don't know much about her background, Scripture tells us she depleted her resources searching for a cure. History describes the humiliating treatments and experimental drugs she endured, only to grow increasingly worse. As she exhausted every possibility, anguish began to choke out hope.

> *"Another day wasted, while I wait on test results. Not one change: I'm still bleeding."*

Yet, that wasn't even the worst part of her illness. Old Testament Law taught that her condition rendered her unclean. Leviticus 25 devotes an entire chapter to the subject. Verses 25–31 share the following:

"'When a woman has a discharge of blood for many days at a time other than her monthly period or has a discharge that continues beyond her period, she will be unclean as long as she has the discharge, just as in the days of her period. Any bed she lies on while her discharge continues will be unclean, as is her bed during her monthly period, and anything she sits on will be unclean, as during her period. Anyone who touches them will be unclean; they must wash their clothes and bathe with water, and they will be unclean till evening. Keep the Israelites separate from things that make them unclean so they will not die in their uncleanness for defiling my dwelling place which is among them."

This was the frame around her disease: she was unclean. Anything she touched was unclean. Anyone who touched her was unclean, requiring a sacrifice to make them acceptable before the Lord. This wasn't simply an annoying menstrual period that went on past seven days. This was a life-altering disease that required a sacrifice, once she stopped bleeding and was considered clean. Except the bleeding never stopped. For 378, 683, 424 seconds, an illness beyond her control controlled her life. Every single instant of every single day, this belief clothed her like a garment: *Don't touch me. I'm unclean.*

No one held her hand through the next inhumane experiment. No one delivered a meal to her front door. No one sat next to her in church, because she wasn't allowed to go. She was cut off from intimacy.

No sexual relations if she was married. No children if she didn't already have them. No human contact without repercussions—for twelve years. She was alone, ashamed, and afraid. My research included a conversation with an acclaimed physician with over 30 years of experience.[19]

What were possible causes of her condition?
Her illness could have been caused by any number of things, including fibroids, compounded by the lack of modern medicine to regulate her periods. Today, we might consider performing a hysterectomy or endometrial ablation to stop the bleeding, depend on test results.

What were her symptoms and complications?
She was emaciated and profoundly anemic from daily hemorrhaging. She lived with overwhelming fatigue, quickly drained by daily activities such as bathing and cooking. She could've developed congestive heart failure, meaning she would become out of breath if she attempted to climb stairs. The loss of bone density left her bones brittle and her joints stiff. Her bone-on-bone pain would have been nearly unbearable as she tried to push her way through the crowd. Severely deficient in minerals, she may have eaten dirt to satisfy her cravings. This disorder, called pica, is even seen today in some third world countries.

What about the psychological and physical ramifications of the lack of touch?
It would've been devastating. We don't even shake a person's hand when they have a cold, much less what she bore. Just a matter of a couple of days of solitary confinement produces debilitating physical symptoms for a prisoner such as headaches, extreme dizziness, and heart palpitations, as well as acute mental and emotional complications such as depression, incoherency, and suicidal thoughts. She was in really bad shape.

The disease took everything. Over and over, the same thoughts plagued her mind:

> *"What is wrong with me? Why can't I get well? What else can I possibly do? What if this never ends?"*

Isolated and out of options, she heard Jesus was in town. Fear listed all the reasons she should stay home. She risked public humiliation and stern rebuke. She risked shattered bones and dashed hopes. Yet, faith found a way. With four words, she stood up to all this disease had cost her: *"If I can just..."* **She stopped rehearsing the familiar tune of the *"what-ifs"* and changed the lyrics to *"if only."***

She wasn't riding into battle to save a king. She wasn't running back to town to save a community. She was crawling through a crowd to save herself. When no one else would fight for her cause, she fearlessly fought for herself. She taught us that, sometimes, we are our own cause.

Most simply refer to her as, "the woman with the issue of blood." The world strips our identity down to the sum total of our issues (and we all have them). Physical and emotional suffering threatens to blur our ability to think clearly and manage life effectively. Pain can cause us to lose sight of God-sized dreams.

> *The loneliness of divorce.*
> *The weariness of illness.*
> *The heaviness of depression.*

But, girls, we can't let issues obscure our calling. We can't let pain pulverize our purpose. If we want to encounter God, we can't do it from the comfort of our couch. **Fear will always list the reasons we can't. Faith finds a way.** Let's choose to be a part of our miracle by redirecting our thoughts through His Word and centering our hearts through His presence. Let's replace our chorus of "what-ifs" with a refrain of "if only." Jesus is the solution to our suffering. She hadn't intended to talk to Him or even let Him know she was there. She was content with the bare minimum at the back of the crowd because she didn't want to bother Him. But an intimate problem required an intimate solution. Amid a sea of people, Jesus felt her touch.

Find Your Fearless

FEARLESS TAKEAWAY

Fear will always list the reasons we can't. Faith finds a way.

FEARLESS NEXT STEPS

1. Pain can cause us to lose sight of our God-sized dreams and pulverize our purpose. As you read about the effects of her condition, what impacted you the most and why?

2. Leviticus 25 devotes an entire chapter to the ramifications and regulations of being "unclean." This belief clothed her like a garment: *Don't touch me. I'm unclean.* Does any false belief keep you isolated from others or afraid of intimacy with Jesus?

3. Faith found a way. She stopped rehearsing the familiar tune of the *"what-ifs"* and changed the lyrics to *"if only."* Is there an area of your life where you need to replace a chorus of "what-ifs" with a refrain of "if only?"

FEARLESS DECLARATION

I refuse to let any issue obscure my calling. Every time I rehearse a "what-if," I will ask the Holy Spirit to help me replace it with an "if only." I will let faith find a way when pain obscures my God-sized dreams. I will fearlessly fight like a girl.

FEARLESS PRAYER

My prayer in my words…

Her Choice—Stand Out

The Sea of Galilee isn't a sea at all. Kinneret, the lowest freshwater lake on earth, is only about 13 miles long and 8 miles wide. It's surrounded by several small towns, including Capernaum, the likely location of our story. Filming here proved challenging due to tight quarters. I can hardly imagine what it must have been like the day Jesus came to town.

The disciples did their best to surround Jesus and pull Him through the swarming crowds. Everywhere they turned, people were grasping for the Healer. As our fearless fighter slowly made her way to the back of the throng of people, a man named Jairus ran to the front and threw himself at Jesus' feet. Their stories collided in the most unexpected of ways.

"When Jesus had again crossed over by boat to the other side of the lake, a large crowd gathered around him while he was by the lake. Then one of the synagogue leaders, named Jairus, came, and when he saw Jesus, he fell at his feet. He pleaded earnestly with him, "My little daughter is dying. Please come and put your hands on her so that she will be healed and live." So Jesus went with him."

Jairus, a prestigious religious leader at the upper end of the political and social spectrum, also found himself completely helpless. Neither pedigree nor position mattered; he just needed Jesus to touch his daughter. With laser focus, the disciples forged ahead on an urgent mission to meet an imminent need.

"Step back! Let the Master through!"

This moment truly began twelve years earlier, when a young, devout Jewish couple celebrated the birth of their baby girl. That same day, across town, a woman of means noticed strange symptoms. As Jairus' daughter grew, sharing milestones and memories, the woman deteriorated from an incurable disease. Luke 8 tells us that his daughter was 12 years of age when Jesus came through Capernaum. Every day this family spent together marked another day this woman bled without reprieve. Just as a despairing mother implored her husband to go *get* Jesus, a desperate woman mustered every ounce of strength to get *to* Him.

She made not one, but three fearless choices in this story. First, she dared to leave her home and brave the crowd. She believed that a moment in God's presence could remedy a lifetime of pain. She stood up for herself and trusted God to fulfill the dreams He planted within her—before illness stripped her bare. Second, she dared to touch Jesus. Her faith rose above the fear of rebuke. She didn't *exactly* touch Jesus: she touched the hem of His garment.

"A large crowd followed and pressed around him. And a woman was there who had been subject to bleeding for twelve years. She had suffered a great deal under the care of many doctors and had spent all she had, yet instead of getting better she grew worse. When she heard about Jesus, she came up behind him in the crowd and touched his cloak, because she thought, "If I just touch his clothes, I will be healed." Immediately her bleeding stopped, and she felt in her body that she was freed from her suffering."

Girls, that means she felt this pain every second of every day. Not a minute went by that she didn't think about it, wondering when she'd wake from this horrific nightmare. She thought her ribs might break as she struggled to shove her way to Jesus. Her eyes darted furiously through the horde of people. And then she saw it: the reminder that she was untouchable. She knew the familiar hue of blue as the tassel swept just above the ground in front of her. She pushed down the fear that gripped her heart and ignored the rocks that dug into her knees. She knew it the instant her frail fingers grabbed ahold of the fringe of His garment: she was miraculously transformed. Jesus accomplished in one moment what no one could do in 12 years.

"At once Jesus realized that power had gone out from him. He turned around in the crowd and asked, "Who touched my clothes?""

A cloak…a hem…His clothes…what exactly did she reach for? I asked esteemed Rev/Rabbi Eric E. Walker to share his insights.

"To the untrained reader, the story of the woman with the issue of blood touching the hem of Jesus' garment and receiving her healing, might conjure up a picture of a robe with a modern-day hem. It would only be fitting for the Messiah to be wearing such a robe that had a neatly finished bottom. However, Jesus was an observant Jewish man who would have followed all the commands of the Mosaic Laws.

In Numbers 15, The LORD said to Moses, "Speak to the people of Israel, and tell them to make tassels on the corners of their garments throughout their generations, and to put a cord of blue on the tassel of each corner. And it shall be a tassel for you to look at and remember all the commandments of the LORD, to do them, not to follow after your own heart and your own eyes, which you are inclined to whore after. So you shall remember and do all my commandments, and be holy to your God. I am the LORD your God, who brought you out of the land of Egypt to be your God: I am the LORD your God."

The commandment is quite clear that these fringes were to be visible so that when you looked upon them you would be reminded of God's Commandments. The fringe was to be placed on each corner of the garment. The word "corner" in Hebrew translates as wings. Therefore, Jesus would have been wearing a 4-cornered garment with tassels or fringe tied to each corner on the exterior, fully visible according to the command."[20]

The garment didn't heal her: her faith made contact with His power. His mind was fixated on a crucial assignment and His body was pressed on every side. Yet, instantaneously, He felt power leave His body. Jesus didn't *send* the power; it was pulled out of Him. Think about it, girls: the faith of a powerless woman drew power from God. She believed nothing was too difficult for God. As she seized the moment, her determination met His.

A group of dumbfounded disciples tried to move Jesus on. After all, this was nothing more than a pesky interruption to the grave situation ahead. I can't help but see myself in them… in my resentment when something poses a distraction to my busy schedule. In my drive to meet a deadline, I may have missed a miracle. They viewed her as an unnecessary disruption, but Jesus regarded her as His highest priority. Insistent, He kept looking around to see who had done it. Of course, He knew who touched Him. He didn't need to know for *His* good; He needed to know for hers. We'll see why in just a moment as we watch her take her final, fearless step.

Perhaps you're hovering precariously in a holding pattern that never seems to end. Maybe adversity has drained the color from your face, or pain has taken the fight out of you. We may feel powerless over our circumstances, but we can still touch Jesus. **Faith pushes the reset button on a stalled life.** We so often reach for other things when we're desperate. Jesus wants to be our first defense, not our last resort. He never grows irritated when we interrupt Him. He never moves us to the bottom of the pile or forgets to call us back. He never tires of listening to us or fails to protect us. No matter what you're pushing through, don't give up. Sometimes God changes our situation, and sometimes He changes us. Either way, our desperation makes way for the miraculous when we touch Jesus.

Find Your Fearless

FEARLESS TAKEAWAY

Faith pushes the reset button on a stalled life.

FEARLESS NEXT STEPS

1. Jesus accomplished in one moment what no one could do in 12 years. Sometimes God changes a situation, and sometimes God changes us. What area of your life desperately needs His transformational touch? Ask Him for renewed perspective as you believe for a miracle.

2. In my drive to meet a deadline, I may have missed a miracle. The disciples viewed her as an unnecessary disruption, but Jesus regarded her as His highest priority. How do you tend to handle interruptions? In what ways does the example of Jesus challenge you to view them differently?

3. We so often reach for other things when we're desperate. Jesus wants to be our first defense, not our last resort. What do you tend to reach for other than Jesus? What's one step you can make to push the reset button in your life?

FEARLESS DECLARATION

I believe God can change my situation and change me in my situation. I will reframe interruptions, so I don't miss divine appointments. When something causes me to feel powerless, I will remember that nothing is too difficult for God.

FEARLESS PRAYER

My prayer in my words…

Her Catalyst for Change—Stand Strong

Not all warriors wear combat boots and camouflage. Some wear hospital gowns and pink ribbons. Not all soldiers fight on the battlefield. Some fight on the front-lines of an addiction recovery support group. Or in a homeless shelter. Or at a dinner table, alone. And some fight the odds to crawl to Jesus and change a culture.

Society told her she didn't belong there. Disease told her she didn't have a chance. Pain told her she no longer had a purpose. Yet, faith triumphed over fear. She entered the fight as an underdog, but she left a champion.

Mark and Luke share the same account, with a slight variance in emphasis. As a physician, Luke was familiar with the experimental drugs she took in vain. His account in Chapter 8:47–48 concludes our story this way: "Then the woman, seeing that she could not go unnoticed, came trembling and fell at his feet. In the presence of all the people, she told why she had touched him and how she had been instantly healed. Then he said to her, "Daughter, your faith has healed you. Go in peace.""

Mark notes, "Then the woman, knowing what had happened to her, came and fell at his feet and, trembling with fear, told him the whole truth. He said to her, "Daughter, your faith has healed you. Go in peace and be freed from your suffering.""

Wait, just a minute. Both writers observed something: she was visibly shaking from fear. Is it paradoxical, then, to deem her "fearless?" Quite the opposite. The very fact that she trembled as she came to Jesus warrants her inclusion in this book. Science explains the physical phenomenon that occurs when fear activates our "fight-or-flight" response:

"This response is governed by the sympathetic nervous system, a division of the peripheral nervous system that consists of nerves that originate in the spinal cord and make connections with diverse body organs. When we are afraid, these nerves send signals to our organs to prepare the body either to flee from or fight a predator or potential threat, increasing the heart rate, dilating the pupils and causing tunnel vision. Trembling might be caused by the release of adrenaline (one of the hormones released during fight-or-flight), which, in the absence of actual fighting or fleeing (when we would be using our muscles), may result in trembling. Or, it could be due to the sudden drop in blood glucose, as glucose is diverted from the blood to the muscles during the fight-or-flight response."[21]

Girls, every fiber of her body reacted to this moment. Her nerves shot off rapid-fire signals and her pulse raced. Her throat closed and her eyes filled. As Jesus waited for an answer to His question, she agonized over her own: *"Should I stay, or should I go?"*

He could've called her out in a heartbeat and put an end to her misery. He could've shrugged it off and continued on His way. It wasn't cruelty that demanded she speak: it was compassion. He wanted a public confession of her faith so He could openly commend her for it. Finally, a frail voice broke through the hushed crowd. *"I touched You, Jesus. It was me."*

She made her third, fearless choice when she refused to let fear keep her silent any longer. Faith found a way. She rose above the doubts that nearly killed her courage and shared her story. The shroud of isolation that suffocated her lifted off the moment she touched the garment that covered Him. She refused to let the reaction of an angry crowd or the rebuff of a Rabbi imprison her one more second. She was no longer trapped inside her own body; she was free.

It's hard to fully appreciate the mercy in the way Jesus treated her without understanding how the Pharisees would've reacted. Jesus didn't recoil in disgust or reprimand her in public. **She didn't make Him unclean; He made her whole.** He not only healed her physical body and restored her dignity; He challenged the belief system of the day. We still refer to her as "the woman with the issue of blood," but Jesus called her "daughter." He lifted off her stigma and honored her faith. She was no longer defined by her issue—she was defined by His touch. Jesus not only freed her from her illness; He clothed her with new identity. Everything changed when her uncommon faith had an unexpected encounter with an extraordinary God.

When everyone else gave up on her, Jesus gave her a second chance. Pain had trapped her for so long, she had all but given up on herself. Girls, her story speaks volumes to our suffering. It speaks to the tender places rubbed raw by pain. It speaks to the issues so stuck to our spirit that we can't separate them from our identity anymore.

When the enemy tempts us to believe...

I am this soul-crushing illness. I'll never beat it.
I am this addiction. I'll never break it.
I am this crippling anxiety. I'll never shake it.
I am this financial disaster. I'll never overcome it.
I am this haunting sadness. I'll never get past it.

Faith fights back.

The gravity of the issues we carry weighs down our ability to see our value. Jesus reminds us that we are worth fighting for. His blood washes away the lies we believe and reaches us wherever we are. He pulls us out of the back of the crowd until we're close enough to touch Him. We can face anything when we're facing Jesus. His presence restores our peace and clothes us with a custom-made identity in Him.

Before Jesus could even finish His sentence, her glorious moment was brusquely cut short. Her heart sank as she heard their words: "Jairus, your daughter is dead. Why bother the teacher anymore?" She realized her miracle came at the expense of his. Perhaps the internal voice of comparison she had listened to for 12 years once again throbbed in her ears: *"Look what you did. Who do you think you are? You're just an ordinary nobody. He's a leader in this community—and now his daughter is gone because of you."*

Jesus heard it all and silenced it with one sentence: *"Don't be afraid; just believe."* While one daughter's miracle was instantaneous, another daughter's miracle was delayed. No boundary or barrier was too difficult for Jesus. He rebuilt one life and resurrected another.

It doesn't matter if we're sitting in the lap of luxury or struggling paycheck to paycheck: we are all helpless without Jesus. He ministers to the hurting places in our own hearts and the places we hurt for others. Whether you're believing for your own miracle or praying for someone else's, no time spent with Jesus is ever wasted. He can handle our hard questions and strengthen our heavy hearts. He hears us when we pray, sustains us when we don't understand, and trains us to fight with purpose.

The sun announced the dawn of another day, and for the first time in 12 years, she wasn't bleeding. Hot tears rolled down both of her cheeks as she embraced her new reality. She took a moment to put her finger on the unfamiliar emotion she felt. Then it hit her: this was peace. She was no longer the woman with the issue of blood…no longer ravaged by illness or battered by comparison. She was the woman with the story everyone wanted to hear.

We can only imagine the days and months that followed, as our fearless fighter reclaimed her purpose in life. She relished her first day back at work and cried all the way through church. She picked up the mirror and saw the light back in her eyes. She held her neighbor's newborn baby and perhaps a suitor's hand. Scripture doesn't share what the rest of her life entailed, but we do know this: no one encounters Jesus and leaves the same.

Find Your Fearless

FEARLESS TAKEAWAY

Faith fights back.

FEARLESS NEXT STEPS

1. Not all warriors wear combat boots and camouflage. What does your fight look like? You may feel like an underdog, but you can emerge a champion. Push your pain into the heart of Jesus as you spend time in His presence.

2. Girls, her story speaks volumes to our suffering. It speaks to the tender places rubbed raw by pain. It speaks to the issues so stuck to our spirit that we can't separate them from our identity anymore. What area of your life needs covered by His custom-made identity? Let His love wash over you and give you the faith to fight back.

3. She took a moment to put her finger on the unfamiliar emotion she felt. Then it hit her: this was peace. Jesus didn't just heal her—He clothed her in peace. Identify any area where fear or anxiety is robbing you of peace. Ask the Holy Spirit to help you rest in the faithfulness of God as you receive His assurance.

FEARLESS DECLARATION

I am a fearless fighter. I can face anything because I'm facing Jesus. I will stop believing the lies of the enemy and clothe myself with my custom-made identity in Christ. Nothing is too difficult for Jesus. He can rebuild one life and resurrect another.

FEARLESS PRAYER

My prayer in my words…

Her Calling and Ours

In a lengthy conversation at a well in Samaria, Jesus displayed His specialty in renovation. He was a one-man clean-up crew, demolition team, and interior designer. He didn't just slap on a fresh coat of paint or buff out a few minor scratch marks. He tore down long-standing beliefs and overhauled a woman's entire life. As He moved through Galilee, He showed us His expertise in restoration, bringing healing and deliverance in an instant. This time, He was a man of few words.

> *"Who touched me?"*
> *"Daughter, your faith has healed you."*
> *"Go in peace and be freed from your suffering."*

Three. That's the number of sentences it took for Jesus to change the life of a woman and challenge the mindset of a culture. In less than two dozen words, Jesus issued a charge to our fearless fighter that drew her out of her private pain and onto a public platform. In her choices, we see the power of our own. We weren't created to live a stuck life, but one saturated with purpose. We experience freedom to walk in our God-given calling when we develop our ability to recognize His voice. We serve as a catalyst for change when we allow Him to change us in His presence. When we respond to Jesus in faith, we'll overcome the barriers that keep us from fearless living.

GET AHOLD OF JESUS

So many things hold us back from pushing through to Jesus. She fought through debilitating pain and demoralizing public opinion. She could've felt so ordinary next to Jairus and wondered why Jesus would even help her when He had more important matters to tend to. Comparison keeps us in the back of the crowd. Insecurity rips at the fabric of our identity and tells us we're unworthy of anything more. Shame hopes Jesus won't see us while we hide behind our issues. Girls, we can win the fight with the "less-than-lies" because Jesus is more than enough.

She initiated her miracle long before she touched the hem of His garment. She stepped out in faith the moment she dared to believe for the impossible. She thought, "If I can just..." Girls, the battle against fear begins in our mind. **When an issue has ahold of us, we need to get ahold of Jesus.** We transform our perspective by spending time in His presence. Worship softens our hardened heart. Prayer aligns our stubborn will. Peace settles our weary spirit. Grace governs our anxious mind. When we're worn out and worn down, the enemy tempts us to self-medicate with short-term solutions that short-cut the will of God. We avoid his dangerous detours by putting our hope in Jesus. We can trust His power to meet us at our point of need. It only takes a moment in God's presence to remedy a lifetime of pain.

GET UNSTUCK

Life doesn't always play nice. When things don't unfold like we think they should, we can become stuck in the quicksand of unmet expectations. Disappointment nips at the heels of an unexpected delay. Resentment creeps in the back door of an endless ordeal. Fear traps us into believing that our issue is too big for God...that we'll never be free from the ache of abandonment or the struggle with identity. Fear tricks us into believing that we're a burden...unloved...invisible. Girls, don't let resentment corrode contentment. No issue is beyond God's power to change it. No wound is beyond God's power to heal it. His strength is made perfect in our weakness and His mercy is greater than our mess.

We can get—and stay—unstuck. Jesus wants us to "be freed from our suffering." It doesn't matter if you're suffering because of something you've done, or because of something done to you: the blood of Jesus covers it all. Judgement says, "You deserve this." Jesus says, "I will take this." When we put our faith in Him, we have nothing to lose but our problems. He is the balm for our brittle emotions and the cure for our cemented thought patterns. He empowers us to extend forgiveness to others and grace to ourselves.

We experience freedom when we embrace surrender. A cold, sterile hospital room seems an unlikely place to discover freedom. Yet, that's the sacred space I encountered an extraordinary God. Girls, I didn't have an ounce of fight left. But what I did have was the choice to surrender. Sometimes, that's the greatest fight of all. No matter what we go through, we are not powerless. We flex our faith muscles through the power of surrender. When we let go of our agenda and grab ahold of God's, He transforms pain into purpose.

GET GOING

Her moment didn't end in the middle of a busy street. Jesus released her with a command: "go in peace." Her miraculous transformation meant the beginning of a new chapter. She went home and rebuilt her life. Those first few days were assuredly mixed with moments of sheer joy and utter angst as she grew in strength. It's easy to feel overwhelmed when you're starting over. Fearless fighters don't give up; they get going. Don't let the dread of demands drain your resolve. If you're struggling to gain traction on a stalled life, just start somewhere.

Stuck in an unfulfilling job? Cultivate that dream you've relegated to the back burner. Take a class and explore some new possibilities. Put feet to that fresh idea and turn it into a small business.

Stuck in a lackluster marriage? Invest quality time and renewed energy into your relationship. Read a marriage-enhancing book together and get away for a couple of nights to reconnect. If the distance is deep, seek counseling to repair the damage and improve communication.

Stuck in a destructive habit? Ask the Holy Spirit to help you develop self-control and set yourself up for success with an accountability partner. Consider enrolling in a program designed to help you move forward into freedom.

Whether you're in a season of renovation or restoration, God's goal is transformation. We give Him our pieces and He gives us peace. Peace is a deep-settled contentment that comes when we completely trust the character of God. Perhaps you're patiently waiting on a promise. Maybe your God-sized dreams look vastly different than you imagined. Peace calms our confusion and centers us in His will. Peace gives us the confidence to walk in God's call on our lives and dare to do extraordinary things.

God doesn't just want to heal us for a moment; He wants to build a relationship for a lifetime. Never underestimate the power of God's' presence. Few people understood this more than David. When issues got ahold of David, David got ahold of God. God convicted David when sin took him off course and comforted him when family turmoil broke his heart. He wrote about many of his experiences in the Book of Psalms, showing us this important truth: presence = relationship. Whether you're restarting a stalled life or waiting on the fulfillment of a promise, let David's words in Psalm 16 remind you that God's got it—and He's got you.

Psalm 16

Keep me safe, my God,
　　for in you I take refuge.
　I say to the Lord, "You are my Lord;
　　apart from you I have no good thing."
I say of the holy people who are in the land,
　　"They are the noble ones in whom is all my delight."
Those who run after other gods will suffer more and more.
　　I will not pour out libations of blood to such gods
　　or take up their names on my lips.
Lord, you alone are my portion and my cup;
　　you make my lot secure.
The boundary lines have fallen for me in pleasant places;
　　surely I have a delightful inheritance.
I will praise the Lord, who counsels me;
　　even at night my heart instructs me.
I keep my eyes always on the Lord.

With him at my right hand, I will not be shaken.
Therefore my heart is glad and my tongue rejoices;
    my body also will rest secure,
because you will not abandon me to the realm of the dead,
    nor will you let your faithful one see decay.
You make known to me the path of life;
    you will fill me with joy in your presence,
    with eternal pleasures at your right hand.

Find Your Fearless

FEARLESS TAKEAWAY

When an issue has ahold of us, we need to get ahold of Jesus.

FEARLESS NEXT STEPS

1. When we're worn out and worn down, the enemy tempts us to self-medicate with short-term solutions that short-cut the will of God. We avoid his dangerous detours by putting our hope in Jesus. Are you fighting a "less-than-lie?" Let Jesus transform your thoughts—He is more than enough.

2. David wrote about many of his experiences in the Book of Psalms, showing us this important truth: presence = relationship. God doesn't just want to heal us for a moment. He wants to build a relationship for a lifetime. What part of Psalm 16 ministered to you the most and why? Consider incorporating the Psalms into your devotional times as you deepen your relationship with the Lord.

3. Fearless fighters don't give up; they get going. If you're struggling to gain traction on a stalled life, just start somewhere. What's one step you can take right now?

FEARLESS DECLARATION

I will fight every "less-than-lie" with the truth of God's Word. I will flex my faith muscles through the power of surrender. I will let go of my agenda and grab ahold of God's. He will make known to me the path I'm to take and fill me with joy in His presence.

FEARLESS PRAYER

My prayer in my words…

Priscilla

Her Story & Our Starting Place

> We can leave a mark on earth
> by making a difference for eternity.

ROMANS 16:3-4, 2 TIMOTHY 4:16-21

Before you begin your study, view the companion video resource here:

 www.angeladonadio.com

I have also included the video message and our key Scripture passage below.

Well, girls, I'm sad to say it, but we have come to the final session of *"Fearless."* I've absolutely loved our time together! As we've studied these ordinary women who dared to do extraordinary things, we've found our fearless in their stories. They weren't a flash in the pan; they were strong catalysts for change. Their fearless faith left footprints for us to follow. A formidable force in their own right, they seized God-moments and shaped cultures. Their purpose was also interwoven with God's greater narrative. They impacted the lives of Moses the Deliverer, Joshua and the Israelites, King David, Jesus, the Savior of the world, and countless more. Our stories aren't written in a vacuum. They're written with the pen of an extraordinary God who takes our ordinary lives and uses them for kingdom purpose.

The woman we're about to meet is no different. She courageously assisted three major leaders of the New Testament. After Jesus' death and resurrection, Christianity advanced through the impact of His disciples and the apostles. Priscilla was the mother of the early church. Her influence is seen in the ministry of the great evangelist, Paul, the powerful preacher, Apollos, and the prominent pastor, Timothy. Two-thirds of the New Testament was written by the apostle Paul, who traveled extensively as a missionary to bring the Gospel to the Gentile world—and she had a crucial role to play. Priscilla was a friend and co-worker to Paul, a teacher to Apollos, and a mentor to Timothy. She wasn't threatened by other people's success or crippled by comparison. And she's one woman I cannot wait to meet in heaven.

Live From Caesarea Maritima

Welcome to Caesarea Maritima, an ancient port and Roman colony on the edge of the Mediterranean Sea. Paul came through here many times on his missionary journeys. It was during his travels to Corinth that he first met Priscilla and her husband Aquila, driven out of Rome by the edict of Claudius against the Jews. Paul lived with them for a year and a half, working together as tentmakers while the church met in their home. Oh, to have had a seat at their kitchen table and hear the rich conversations about theology and ministry.

She is mentioned in six different passages of Scripture, always alongside her husband and ministry partner, Aquila. How I wish we knew their love story. But we do know Priscilla was a hard-working businesswoman, a co-laborer alongside Paul in the church, and loyal to the point of risking her life for him.

Romans 16:3–4 tells us: "Greet Priscilla and Aquila, my co-workers in Christ Jesus. They risked their lives for me. Not only I but all the churches of the Gentiles are grateful to them. Greet also the church that meets at their house."

In Acts 24–26, here in Caesarea Maritima, he made his defense and shared the message of the Gospel in chains one last time before Governor Festus and King Agrippa sent him to Rome. Languishing in a cold dungeon, Paul said his final goodbye in a letter he wrote to Timothy and the church he loved in Ephesus. In the last book he would ever write before being beheaded under the cruel Emperor Nero, he penned these words:

2 Timothy 4:16–21

"At my first defense, no one came to my support, but everyone deserted me. May it not be held against them. But the Lord stood at my side and gave me strength, so that through me the message might be fully proclaimed, and all the Gentiles might hear it. And I was delivered from the lion's mouth. The Lord will rescue me from every evil attack and will bring me safely to his heavenly kingdom. To him be glory for ever and ever. Amen. Greet Priscilla and Aquila and the household of Onesiphorus. Erastus stayed in Corinth, and I left Trophimus sick in Miletus. Do your best to get here before winter. Eubulus greets you, and so do Pudens, Linus, Claudia and all the brothers and sisters. The Lord be with your spirit. Grace be with you all."

Please don't miss this. In his deep loneliness and heartache, he wrote down the names of those who meant the most to him; those who stood with him to the end. One of those names is Priscilla. She fiercely protected the Gospel at all cost—and we are here because of it.

<><><><><><><><><><><><><><><><><><><><><><><><><><><><><><><>

I can still smell the salt air and feel the wind whipping off the Mediterranean Sea, the closest I could get to Priscilla. Paul racked up more frequent flyer miles than I'll see in a lifetime, jet-setting around the world with a global mission. (Just trace his journeys and see how quickly you get dizzy.) The man who brought the Gospel to the known Gentile world did it in part due to Priscilla and Aquila.

Priscilla lived all over the place, but she never spent a day in a comfort zone. Up against culture and constantly in danger, she turned her home, her marriage, and her career into ministry. She knew she was called, not just to climb the corporate ladder, but to carry the Gospel wherever she went. Her presence left a mark. The open immorality around her didn't scare her, but the thought of people dying without hearing about Jesus did. Her story reminds us that we, too, can find our voice in a loud world. As you pack your bags to travel with Priscilla, tuck these questions into your carry-on:

What if we left the safety of our comfort zone to step into our calling?

What if we cared more about our culture than criticized it?

What if we chose compassion over competition?

We can leave a mark on earth by making a difference for eternity. Priscilla invites us to love without limits and dare to do extraordinary things.

We can leave
a mark on earth
by MAKING A
DIFFERENCE
for eternity.

Her Cause—Stand Up

Priscilla put the final touches on her last order and realized she was late closing shop—again. She draped an olive-green cover over her reliable loom and thanked it for another hard day's work. She wasn't the only one to catch the rumblings coming from her stomach.

"Did you ever eat today?" Aquila planted a quick kiss on her forehead and secured the front door for the night.

"I'll be right inside," Priscilla responded unconvincingly. She chuckled at his knowing glance. *"I promise. I just need to take a quick inventory of supplies."*

Business had trickled in those first couple weeks after moving from Rome. But now, she could barely keep up with demand. She hadn't wanted to leave, and her heart ached for the people she loved back home. Painful remnants of the religious persecution that uprooted their lives still lingered. Yet, she knew without a shadow of a doubt God brought them to Corinth. It wasn't just the thriving tent-making operation that kept them busy; it was life with Paul. Six months earlier, he arrived at their doorstep with a handful of tools and extensive expertise in crafting leather. However, a rough season of discouragement had rubbed his own, thick skin raw.

"I know it's risky to take him in." She leaned forward and propped both elbows on the table. *"Aquila, we'd be harboring a depleted pastor on the run, not to mention the added household expenses. But it's not our first time living dangerously for the Gospel, and you know it won't be the last. I truly believe we have to seize this moment."*

"Absolutely, Priscilla," her husband replied, without a twinge of hesitation. *"Whatever he needs. He's going to have his hands full starting a church in this city, that's for sure. The least we can do is offer him a place to stay and give him an opportunity to work. I'll go get him."*

Priscilla picked up from dinner as he turned to leave.

"You know what this is, don't you?" he asked, with that familiar twinkle in his eye.

"Yes." Her hands clenched firmly around the rim of her plate. *"A divine appointment."*

They didn't wear capes or leap tall buildings in a single bound. But make no mistake: you've just met a trifecta of New Testament superheroes. They fearlessly fought for the lost as they carried the Gospel into some of the most difficult parts of the world. Luke records Paul's missionary journeys in the book of Acts, and introduces us to the dynamic duo of Priscilla and Aquila in Chapter 18.

"After this, Paul left Athens and went to Corinth. There he met a Jew named Aquila, a native of Pontus, who had recently come from Italy with his wife Priscilla, because Claudius had ordered all Jews to leave Rome. Paul went to see them, and because he was a tentmaker as they were, he stayed and worked with them. Every Sabbath he reasoned in the synagogue, trying to persuade Jews and Greeks."

Two little words, *"after this,"* deserve some backstory. A series of disheartening ministry stops drove Paul to Corinth. Bruised at Philippi, persecuted in Berea, and mocked in Athens, he entered the sprawling metropolis as a total stranger. He quickly discovered Priscilla and Aquila in his search for work, possibly by chance, but more likely by reputation.

Most scholars believe that Priscilla was a Gentile from the Roman upper class. She married Aquila, a Jew from the Turkish province of Pontus. Scripture always mentions them together and lists her first in prominence in 3 of the 6 references. In stark contrast to the couple we previously studied, Abigail and Nabal, they lovingly lived, worked, and served side by side. In Rome, they ran a successful business and worked with the apostle Peter in his evangelism efforts. They were expelled around 51 A.D. by the emperor, Claudius, the third Caesar in succession after Augustus and Tiberius. Originally, he treated the Jews favorably, but eventually caved to pressure from outside parties. As hostility mounted, Priscilla mourned. After countless sleepless nights beseeching God to intervene, she packed up her entire life and settled as a refugee in Corinth, the nearest major city outside of Italy.

Priscilla had no control over the political climate that demanded a do-over. She could've easily stuffed a suitcase full of bitterness and anger. Spent from months of sacrifice and sorrow, she could've slammed the door in Paul's face. Instead, she chose to remain faithful to God and work tirelessly beside her husband to restart their business. The Roman government housed its military in leather tents all over the empire, securing a means for their work to expand through branches in Rome, Corinth, and eventually, Ephesus.

She trusted God to not only provide financial security, but to fill the emptiness she felt after letting go of her ministry in Rome. She wasn't about to let a thin layer of disappointment come between her and her relationship with God. **She understood that sometimes God's hardest *no* is our greatest *yes*.** He interrupted her ordinary routine in the most extraordinary of ways. She and Aquila quickly discerned the obvious: God used the cruel mandate of a wicked leader to get them exactly where He wanted them. For nearly eighteen months, their home served as a haven for Paul and a meeting place for the church that grew under his leadership. The three co-laborers rallied around the same cause: get the Gospel to Corinth. This was no modest vision considering the city of 700,000, one of the greatest in the Roman Empire, was also one of the most corrupt on the planet.

Strategically located on a thin strip of land between the Mediterranean and Aegean Seas, Corinth served as a major trade route and home to a mixed population of Romans, Greeks, and Jews. It was a melting pot of Greek mythology, rampant cult activity, and unbridled immorality. The Greeks created the word, "*korinthiazesthai*: to live like a Corinthian," to represent someone who was completely morally bankrupt.[22] Early on, Priscilla and Aquila did their best to prepare Paul for what he would witness as they toured the city.

> Priscilla's eyes brimmed with tears.
> "Paul, I could scarcely believe it the first time I saw the Temple

of Aphrodite. Even though it's basically in ruins, the incense-filled monument to the worship of the goddess of beauty, pleasure, and fertility, employs more than 1000 "priestess prostitutes" that work around the clock in "church-run brothels." Day and night, sailors, Greek males, and foreigners travel from far and wide to engage in sexual activity all around the temple in the hopes of gaining favor from the goddess. I found out that some of the girls, no more than 12 years years of age, were purchased by status-seeking Greek athletes and offered to Aphrodite as sex slaves.

Then there's the temple of Poseidon, where they hold the Isthmian Games. They believe he rules the sea, which is so crucial to commerce here, and think he's responsible for the frequent earthquakes. Paul, so many vile things are done to appease him. The people here are so confused…they even have a temple they call the "Pantheon: All the gods." You know the Roman cults to Isis and Mithras. They've infiltrated here, too, with their promise of wisdom and understanding.

Just a ways down the hill is a shrine dedicated to Asklepios, the god of healing, and his daughter, Hygieia. Sick people come from everywhere to stand and pray in front of clay replicas of body parts hung around the temple. Paul, this city is desperate for the Gospel. I know this won't be an easy place to plant a church, but we have to find a way to stand up against all of this. Whatever we have—our home, our resources, our time—it's yours."

In Priscilla and Aquila, Paul found business partners, ministry co-laborers, and the truest of friends. They stayed loyal through his constant travels. They assisted him in his frequent times of need. They loved him through excruciating bouts of loneliness. Priscilla didn't have it all figured out when Paul showed up at their door. But what she did have was a cause: The Gospel. Undaunted by the arduous terrain in front of her, she stood up for it everywhere she went. More than anything, she wanted

God to use her. She and Aquila became one of the strongest influences on the apostle Paul. And God's hardest no became their greatest yes.

We have the proof of their investment as they sought to change what it meant to be called "a Corinthian." The New Testament contains 13 books by Paul, and the longest is his combined letter to the Corinthians. It stands as a testament to the tough task taken on by our superheroes. Paul addresses key issues in the first century church—still just as prevalent today. Soak in his first few words to the church they planted:

"To the church of God in Corinth, to those sanctified in Christ Jesus and called to be his holy people, together with all those everywhere who call on the name of our Lord Jesus Christ—their Lord and ours: Grace and peace to you from God our Father and the Lord Jesus Christ.

I always thank my God for you because of his grace given you in Christ Jesus. For in him you have been enriched in every way—with all kinds of speech and with all knowledge— God thus confirming our testimony about Christ among you. Therefore, you do not lack any spiritual gift as you eagerly wait for our Lord Jesus Christ to be revealed. He will also keep you firm to the end, so that you will be blameless on the day of our Lord Jesus Christ. God is faithful, who has called you into fellowship with his Son, Jesus Christ our Lord."

Sometimes we pray until we think our hearts might just break, only to find ourselves facing a do-over. It doesn't mean God doesn't love us, or that we've somehow veered disastrously off course. It means God loves us enough to say no when denial protects our calling. He's not unkind; He's intentional. Unexpected encounters often come through undone moments. We don't always see how God uses the worst of circumstances to bring out the best in us. We're often blind to the way He orchestrates events to ensure we land smack dab in the middle of His will. He strategically places us and meticulously shapes us for maximum kingdom impact. And beautiful girl, your obedience will determine your influence.

Priscilla let God shape her character because she cared more about *calling* than *comfort*. She isn't a fictional crusader splashed across the pages of a comic book, brought to life by someone's imagination. She may sound like a superhero, but she's a real, ordinary woman, made extraordinary by her faith in God. Grab your passport as we continue her epic journey. You might be okay without your seasickness patch as we sail the choppy waters ahead. But if you truly want to follow her lead, be sure you pack two things: a willingness to obey God at all costs and a heart that loves people without limits.

Find Your Fearless

FEARLESS TAKEAWAY

Sometimes God's hardest no is our greatest yes.

FEARLESS NEXT STEPS

1. Priscilla had no control over the political climate that took her to Corinth. She could've easily stuffed a suitcase full of bitterness and anger. She could've slammed the door in Paul's face, spent from months of sacrifice and sorrow. In what way is God asking you to let go of fear and open your life to others? What do you have that you can share?

2. In what way does the culture of Corinth remind you of your own? How did his words from 1st Corinthians impact you considering the description of the city? Consider reading more of Paul's letter in 1st and 2nd Corinthians.

3. God loves us enough to say no when denial protects our calling. He isn't unkind; He's intentional. If you're facing a do-over, consider how God might be strategically placing you and meticulously shaping you for maximum kingdom purpose.

FEARLESS DECLARATION

I will let God shape me so He can place me wherever He can use me most. I refuse to let a thin layer of disappointment come between me and God. I believe His hardest no can be my greatest yes. I will fearlessly open my life to others and stand up for the cause of Christ anywhere I go.

FEARLESS PRAYER

My prayer in my words…

Her Choice—Stand Out

"Come on, Priscilla. We have to go. Paul is already at the port. They'll be fine—you trained them well."

She sensed the urgency in Aquila's voice and rushed through the end of her instructions. She took one last look around the shop and said her goodbyes. It seemed like only yesterday they had painstakingly set up the fledgling store. Now, only eighteen months later, they were moving again. She felt confident the thriving business was in capable hands. As she closed the door, she let out an audible gasp. Lining both sides of the street were the members of their church. One look at Aquila's face let her know he had arranged the surprise.

They were all there: the girls she rescued from the brothels and the Jews Aquila led to salvation…the women she mentored and the children they loved. Familiar pangs of grief stabbed through the scar she carried following their abrupt exit from Rome. Her heart was ready, though, to partner with Paul in his missionary endeavors. Come what may, they were all in. Aquila had said it best just days earlier: "We're not glued to a place; we're glued to the Gospel."

She shed tears of gratitude as Corinth faded into the distance on the open sea. Privately, she wondered if they were up to the challenge of leading a church without Paul. The thought of him going on to Syria and leaving them in Ephesus overwhelmed her. A stiff breeze lifted the words of Moses as she exhaled a simple prayer into the night sky.

"Lord, you have been our dwelling place throughout all generations. Before the mountains were born or you brought forth the whole world, from everlasting to everlasting you are God. May the favor of the Lord our God rest on us; establish the work of our hands for us. Amen."

Priscilla sailed out of her comfort zone and chartered a course further into her calling with three critical choices: she traveled, she trained, and she took on the temple.

SHE TRAVELED

Acts 18:18–23 records the second do-over by our fearless couple, this time without the covering of Paul. "Paul stayed on in Corinth for some time. Then he left the brothers and sisters and sailed for Syria, accompanied by Priscilla and Aquila. They arrived at Ephesus, where Paul left Priscilla and Aquila." We can't be sure if Paul started a church here during his first missionary journey, but we're positive he trusted Priscilla and Aquila to lead one. He admired their zeal that drove them to care more about a culture than to criticize it. He respected their passion that moved them to offer every area of their lives for the kingdom. Not once had they compartmentalized their home, marriage, or ministry. Make no mistake: this set-apart couple was sold-out for Christ.

Ephesus was the second-most important city in the Roman Empire, with a large Jewish population. Centrally located on the coast of Asia Minor (modern day Turkey), it attracted many high-profile Christian leaders as the Gospel spread across major urban areas. Priscilla and Aquila, alongside the likes of Paul, Timothy, and John, turned a principal commercial metropolis into a foremost center for evangelism. And that, girls, was no small feat.

Her time in Rome under the tutelage of Peter, and her partnership with Paul in Corinth, prepared her for the arduous task before her. Although she wasn't a novice anymore, she needed fresh insight and careful strategy to navigate the city famed for the Temple of Artemis, also called Diana. The behemoth that defined the culture took 120 years to build and boasted over 100 marble pillars, each 7 stories high. She felt so small standing in front of it...so insignificant. Without God's guidance and empowerment, she was helpless against this monstrous maze of gods and goddesses. For weeks on end, she and Aquila prayed for breakthrough, fasting and praying until the wee hours of the morning. As the church began to grow, they traveled once again—this time, across town to hear a preacher named Apollos.

SHE TRAINED

"Meanwhile a Jew named Apollos, a native of Alexandria, came to Ephesus. He was a learned man, with a thorough knowledge of the Scriptures. He had been instructed in the way of the Lord, and he spoke with great fervor and taught about Jesus accurately, though he knew only the baptism of John. He began to speak boldly in the synagogue. When Priscilla and Aquila heard him, they invited him to their home and explained to him the way of God more adequately." Acts 18:24—28.

Although Apollos was a brilliant and commanding preacher, he was hindered by his limited knowledge of the finished work of Jesus Christ on the cross. They modeled their response after Paul's motto: care enough to correct in love. They quickly assessed he was eloquent but misguided and offered to come alongside of him to ensure his ministry was of the utmost effectiveness. They welcomed him into their home, training him in private for what God intended to do in public. Priscilla taught out of the limelight so Apollos could shine in the spotlight. Girls, she chose compassion over competition. She's not criticized by Luke or Paul for teaching a man—she's *commended* for it. In a male dominated environment, Paul elevated her position by calling her a "fellow worker," an equal partner in ministry. She wasn't limited by gender and neither are we.

Steeped in the Word, she was skilled in leading those to Christ who were deceived by the popular religious competitors of the day. She stood out because she wasn't hampered by insecurity or tempted to jockey for position. She and Aquila invested *every single space* of real estate they owned into the kingdom: physical, relational, intellectual, emotional, and financial. Nothing was off limits because they loved without limits. Their devoted influence altered the destiny of Apollos.

Propelled by their invaluable training, Apollos became one of the most renowned preachers and respected apostles of the New Testament. Acts 18:28 tells us, "He vigorously refuted his Jewish opponents in public debate, proving from Scriptures that Jesus was the Messiah." As he zigzagged across the region, he built on the foundation laid in Corinth and returned to Ephesus with Paul. An ordinary encounter produced extraordinary results because Priscilla and Aquila seized the opportunity to impart wisdom, and Apollos allowed them to edit his life.

SHE TOOK ON THE TEMPLE

During Paul's final missionary journey, he came off the road for three years to focus on Ephesus. The ministry had taken its toll, and few others could empathize like our close-knit band of friends. He penned letters to the Corinthians during his stay, sharing this in Chapter 16:19: "Aquila and Priscilla greet you warmly in the Lord, and so does the church that meets at their house." They took on the formidable opponent of the temple of Artemis, perhaps prompting these words in Chapter 4:7–12: "But we have this treasure in jars of clay to show that this all-surpassing power is from God and not from us. We are hard pressed on every side, but not crushed; perplexed, but not in despair; persecuted, but not abandoned; struck down, but not destroyed."

The inhabitants of Ephesus believed that the goddess, Artemis, served as the protector of the city and the provider of wealth. Empowered by the Holy Spirit, Priscilla served as the protector of the Gospel and the provider of freedom. The demonic stronghold proved no match for our fearless trio, who systematically dismantled its control over the people. Acts 19 records the riot that eventually took place as a result of their stand for Christ. A silversmith named Demetrius started an uproar over the mass conversions that depleted his business. Paul's evangelistic efforts resulted in far fewer people purchasing items to use as offerings for the pagan gods. Demetrius called together an array of tradesmen, inciting them to action.

The enraged group of artisans dragged Paul's traveling companions into the amphitheater that held 25,000 people, the notorious site where Paul preached about Christ. He desperately wanted to make an appeal before the angry mob, but his disciples refused, begging him not to venture into the fray. For hours, the rowdy crowd shouted, *"Great is Artemis of the Ephesians!"* until the city clerk finally quieted the chaos and dismissed the assembly.

You might wonder; where were Priscilla and Aquila? Fast forward a few years, and you'll discover a potential clue. In 57 A.D., Claudius lifted his edict against the Jews, and our world-travelers, Priscilla and Aquila, returned to Rome for a short season. During that window of time, Paul wrote the book of Romans while in Corinth, sharing this in Chapter 16:3–4: "Greet Priscilla and Aquila, my co-workers in Christ Jesus. They risked their lives for me. Not only I but all the churches of the Gentiles are grateful to them." Other translations put it this way: "For my life's sake they submitted their own throats to the knife."

No one knows for sure what perilous circumstance prompted Paul to transcribe those words. But evidence supports the belief that our dynamic duo nearly lost their lives in the riot at Ephesus. We don't need to know where they stared down martyrdom for Paul's sake to recognize this: *Priscilla and Aquila were his heroes.*

Our call to heroism may not look quite so dramatic. We may never run headfirst into a danger-filled amphitheater to guard an influential leader like Paul. We might not leave our imprint on a preacher like Apollos, who led untold multitudes to Christ. **We don't have to be iconic to be brave: we just have to be available.** We kick fear to the curb every time we travel uncharted waters to pursue God's call. We protect the cause of the Gospel when we care enough to correct in love or let someone edit our life. We realize our purpose each time we take on a God-given cause. Perhaps you're feeling painfully small as you stand in front of a ridiculously impossible situation. God hears our simple prayers as we believe for breakthrough. Ground yourself in the Word, beautiful girl—and you, too, will stand out for God.

Find Your Fearless

FEARLESS TAKEAWAY

We don't have to be iconic to be brave: we just have to be available.

FEARLESS NEXT STEPS

1. She felt so small standing in front of the Temple to Artemis...so insignificant. She prayed and fasted, asking for the Holy Spirit's guidance and empowerment. What is your greatest impossibility? Where do you most need breakthrough?

2. Priscilla taught out of the limelight so Apollos could shine in the spotlight. She chose compassion over competition. Consider their examples. How is God calling you to "care enough to correct in love"? Who has permission to "edit your life" for the kingdom?

3. We may never run headfirst into a danger-filled amphitheater to guard an influential leader like Paul. We might not leave our imprint on a preacher like Apollos, who led untold multitudes to Christ. We don't have to be iconic to be brave: we just have to be available. List 3 ways you sense God asking you to stand out and leave a mark for Him,

FEARLESS DECLARATION

I will resist the urge to jockey for position and trust God to make a way when there doesn't seem to be one. I will choose compassion over competition as I care enough to speak the truth in love and let godly women speak into my life. I realize God is only asking me to be available: He will do the impossible.

FEARLESS PRAYER

My prayer in my words...

Her Catalyst for Change—Stand Strong

Priscilla and Aquila, the ordinary pair that started as political refugees, ended as one of the principal power couples in all of Scripture. They personified teamwork, choosing to *complete* one another rather than *compete* with one another. They lived as equals: suffering exile together, working together, and co-pastoring a church together. Their kitchen table became hallowed ground for weary itinerant preachers and betrothed couples in need of counsel. Priscilla entertained constant company, poured into her husband, maintained a business, and faced relentless risk to spread the Gospel. They filled their passports with divine assignments, and their calendar with divine appointments.

And everywhere she went, Priscilla carried that burgeoning suitcase crammed with hats. After all, she never knew which one she might need to wear. Some days, she changed by the hour…

Spiritual mother
Teacher
Evangelist
Missionary
Businesswoman
Church planter
Devoted wife
Mover and shaker
Trusted friend

She made a mark on earth by making a difference for eternity. A fearless force for the Gospel, she endured persecution in Rome, opposition in Corinth, and hostility in Ephesus. She refused to let the messiness of ministry and the demands of daily living keep people at arm's length. She served as a catalyst for change alongside a like-minded group of leaders that defended the Gospel at all cost. Her influence is intertwined with the timeless legacies of Paul, Apollos, and Timothy.

In the 28 mentions of Timothy in the New Testament, Paul refers to him as beloved son, brother, companion, co-worker, and a man of God. Timothy grew up under the encouragement of strong women who led him to faith after they heard the Gospel during Paul's first missionary journey to the area. Paul commended Timothy's mother, Eunice, and grandmother, Lois, for instilling in him an intense love for the Scriptures. On Paul's return visit, he received such strong testimony of Timothy's knowledge and disposition, he invited him to join him as a missionary. He became Paul's protégé, and Paul became his spiritual father. Reserved in nature and frequently ill, Timothy was bolstered by his companions and partners in ministry, Priscilla and Aquila.

In A.D. 65, Paul wrote his "last will" in two letters to Timothy while imprisoned in a Roman dungeon. In the closing verses, he expressed heartfelt appreciation to a distinct list of people, including our dynamic duo: "Greet Priscilla and Aquila and the household of Onesiphorus." Onesiphorus lived in Ephesus but visited Paul in Rome on more than one occasion to bring supplies and lift his spirits. Having left Rome for the second time, our power couple was back at the church in Ephesus, working with Paul's "son in the faith," Timothy. They stopped everything the moment the letters arrived.

> The sweet scent of olive oil wafted into the warm, night air. The oil lamps barely provided enough light for them to see, but no one wanted to wait until dawn to read it. Priscilla immediately recognized Paul's trademark insignia and handed the letter to Timothy to read aloud. *"Paul, an apostle of Christ Jesus by the command of God our Savior and of Christ Jesus our hope, to Timothy my true son in the faith: Grace, mercy and peace from God the Father and Christ Jesus our Lord..."*
>
> Fifteen years. It had been fifteen years since he had first shown up on their doorstep. She closed her eyes and pictured the writing desk she and Aquila bought for him in Corinth. Never one to stand

down from a fight, he tried his best to get it on the ship, to no avail. Aquila gripped her hand tight as her tears fell without reservation. She remembered how animated Paul got when he told people the story about meeting Jesus on the Damascus road…and how dark his countenance became when he spoke of overseeing the stoning of Stephen. Grace had made the difference in *all* their lives. Jesus: He was everything.

They had loved without thought of consequence and given without thought of cost. None of them cared who got the glory— that was just the way of an "others-minded life." As Timothy received Paul's impassioned pleas for him to visit, his voice broke with emotion. He carefully handed the letter to Aquila to finish as Priscilla instinctively bowed her head. With heavy hearts, they received the charge from their dearest of friends:

"Preach the word; be prepared in season and out of season; correct, rebuke and encourage—with great patience and careful instruction. For the time will come when people will not put up with sound doctrine. Instead, to suit their own desires, they will gather around them a great number of teachers to say what their itching ears want to hear. They will turn their ears away from the truth and turn aside to myths. But you, keep your head in all situations, endure hardship, do the work of an evangelist, discharge all the duties of your ministry.

For I am already being poured out like a drink offering, and the time for my departure is near. I have fought the good fight, I have finished the race, I have kept the faith. Now there is in store for me the crown of righteousness, which the Lord, the righteous Judge, will award to me on that day—and not only to me, but also to all who have longed for his appearing."

Paul sensed his time had come. Unfortunately, he wasn't wrong. In 68 A.D., he was beheaded in Rome, dying as a martyr for his faith in Jesus Christ. History tells us that it's highly plausible Timothy was present to witness his execution. After Timothy visited Paul in Rome, he returned to Ephesus where he continued to govern the church. Beneath his quiet exterior beat the heart of a lion. Decades of unwavering faith in an extraordinary God culminated in a heroic stand for the cause of Christ. In 97 A.D., 30 years after the death of his beloved mentor, Paul, an 80-year-old Timothy attempted to stop a procession in honor of the goddess Diana. As droves joined to celebrate by carrying masked images and weapons of every kind, his exasperation with their incessant idolatry compelled him to intervene.

They beat him unmercifully and left his body on the spot where they murdered him, until some of his disciples came and carried his broken, bloody frame. Girls, we won't know for sure until we meet them in heaven, but it's possible Priscilla and Aquila helped lay him to rest at the top of a mountain nearby. They loved him in life and may have cared for him in death. We'll also have to wait until heaven to hear the end of Priscilla and Aquila's love story. But most historians share that they, too, were martyred for their faith.

*Priscilla...Aquila...Paul...Apollos...Timothy...*the dream team shared in the sacrifice of it all, so they shared in the result of it all. They join the ranks of countless missionaries who have trekked in their footsteps to fearlessly take the Gospel of Jesus Christ to every corner of the earth. They are among those listed in Hebrews 11:35–40: "There were others who were tortured, refusing to be released so that they might gain an even better resurrection. Some faced jeers and flogging, and even chains and imprisonment. They were put to death by stoning; they were sawed in two; they were killed by the sword. They went about in sheepskins and goatskins, destitute, persecuted and mistreated— the world was not worthy of them. They wandered in deserts and mountains, living in caves and in holes in the ground. These were all commended for their faith, yet none of them received what had been promised, since God had planned something better for us so that only together with us would they be made perfect."

God calls us to love like Priscilla, an ordinary woman who changed the climate of every culture in which she lived. **Her superpower was her uncommon faith in an extraordinary God.** When we filter our choices through the lens of eternity, we shift the atmosphere around us. When we invite the Holy Spirit to manage our calendar, we never miss a God-appointment. In Ephesus, Priscilla brushed shoulders with John, the beloved disciple of Jesus. While exiled on the isle of Patmos for his faith, he penned the book of Revelation. Chapter 11:11 contains the description—and the reward—of every fearless man or woman who chooses to follow Christ no matter what the cost.

"They triumphed over him by the blood of the Lamb and by the word of their testimony; they did not love their lives as to shrink from death."

This, girls. This is what it looks like to be fearless.

Find Your Fearless

FEARLESS TAKEAWAY

Our superpower is our uncommon faith in an extraordinary God.

FEARLESS NEXT STEPS

1. Priscilla refused to let the messiness of ministry and the demands of daily living keep people at arm's length. What tends to prevent you from living an "others-minded life"? Consider ways your relationships might improve by choosing to "complete" instead of "compete."

2. Paul wrote with certainty in 2nd Timothy 4: "I have fought the good fight, I have finished the race, I have kept the faith." His words surely strengthened Timothy to endure hardship and preach sound doctrine even when some didn't want to hear it. How can you take what you've learned from the lives of this dream team to make an impact in your world today?

3. Priscilla was an ordinary woman who changed the climate of every culture in which she lived. She filled her passport with divine assignments and her calendar with divine appointments. Invite the Holy Spirit to manage your calendar. How might your priorities need to shift in order to follow God's call to your fullest potential?

FEARLESS DECLARATION

I will look for ways to use my strengths to "complete" those around me. I will fight the good fight, finish my race, and keep the faith. I will let the Holy Spirit manage my calendar and guide me through every God-assignment. I will leave a mark on earth by making a difference for eternity.

FEARLESS PRAYER

My prayer in my words...

Her Calling and Ours

When the concept for *"Fearless"* was in its infancy, I had all kinds of ideas about how it might turn out. Girls—these women exceeded every expectation. I knew I wanted to cover some of the *"Best Supporting Actresses"* of the Bible—women we knew less about than some of their contemporaries. My early research contributed a loose framework around their list of accomplishments but provided only a glimpse into their personalities. The more I studied, the more I discovered about the unique challenges they faced. The more I prayed, the more I received insight from the Holy Spirit about the distinct role they played. I pored over historical records of each time period and examined countless commentaries and theological perspectives. I filled notebooks to the brim with descriptors and details. And something became abundantly clear: *there was nothing ordinary about these women.*

"Ordinary" is defined as *"under normal conditions; unremarkable; common."*

Yet, in the pages of this resource, part study—part story, we've met women with character traits so rare, we struggled to pick our jaw up off the floor. We've witnessed events so mind-boggling, we stood in awe at God's plan. These women taught us how to stand up in uncommon ways for the common good. They showed us how to stand out with confidence in a fog of uncertainty. They displayed what it looks like to stand strong as a source of immeasurable value to the kingdom of God. They were fearless women who dared to do extraordinary things, because they grounded themselves in the Word instead of the world.

In over two decades of ministry, my husband and I have fielded these questions more than any other:

> *"How do I know what I'm called to do?"*
> *"How do I know if this is the will of God?"*

I felt it only fitting to conclude our time together by providing a composite sketch of the myriad of answers we've given throughout the years. You'll find your voice in a loud world as you discover your cause and *pursue* your calling. You'll seize God-moments to make culture-shaping choices as you *protect* your calling. And you'll embrace God-sized dreams to serve as a catalyst for change as you *practice* your calling. Together, we will rise above the doubts that kill our courage, stop the cycle of comparison, and find our fearless.

YOUR CAUSE—PURSUE YOUR CALLING

Paul is the most prolific writer of the New Testament, and verses from his letters frame our final section. The author of Hebrews remains unknown. Although some attribute it to Paul, still others assert it is the work of Priscilla. (*Add that to your list of notable items we'll learn in heaven.*) Regardless, she was a woman of incomparable influence whose example inspires us to pursue our calling.

> *"Therefore, holy brothers and sisters, who share in the heavenly calling, fix your thoughts on Jesus, whom we acknowledge as our apostle and high priest,"* (Hebrews 3:1)

We recognize our calling in several ways. God shapes us through our relationship with Him. As we spend time in prayer, study His Word, and seek godly counsel, we train our ear to hear His voice. Each one of us has a natural bent toward an area of talent or gifting. Recognizing how God has wired you and realizing what you feel most passionate about provides direction. However, calling isn't limited to natural strengths. It includes spiritual gifts and the unique landscape of our personal experiences. We capitalize on strengths and minimize weaknesses through preparation.

The calling of many Old and New Testament leaders involved extensive periods of preparation. Moses, Elijah, Esther, John the Baptist, Paul, and even Jesus, submitted to seasons which refined their character and aligned their calling.

During this critical groundwork phase, we commit ourselves to training, acquiring knowledge and wisdom for the tasks ahead. Yet, even in those *"backside of the mountain"* times in our lives, those moments when we wrestle with feelings of insignificance, we can begin to step out in small ways.

God crystallizes our calling as we exercise our faith. As we begin to flesh it out, we often start with a wide funnel. The Holy Spirit guides us to narrow our focus to the places our contribution provides the most value. Before I ever first set foot on the African continent, I sensed a God-given passion for her people. I discerned His "yes" for my first trip, assisting in kids camps and village ministry. A series of God-appointments paved the way for many subsequent journeys. In those early days, I didn't fully understand what God intended to do through my heart for Africa. Now, as the founder of *"Voice of the Voiceless,"* I work closely with rural women across the continent, empowering them through micro-enterprise opportunities and the message of the Gospel. As an advocate for those who often cannot speak for themselves, I work in remote parts of Africa and around the world. **Baby steps become God-leaps through obedience.** Pursue your calling with confidence. Take that first step and trust God to lead the way.

YOUR CHOICE—PROTECT YOUR CALLING

"As a prisoner for the Lord, then, I urge you to live a life worthy of the calling you have received. Be completely humble and gentle; be patient, bearing with one another in love. Make every effort to keep the unity of the Spirit through the bond of peace. There is one body and one Spirit, just as you were called to one hope when you were called; one Lord, one faith, one baptism; one God and Father of all, who is over all and through all and in all," (Ephesians 4:1–6)

Following God's call isn't always easy: it requires sacrifice and exacts a cost. The excitement of the "honeymoon phase" of our calling can fade when turbulence hits. We can navigate the normal process of growth pains by making necessary adjustments, maintaining a healthy attitude, and relying completely on the Holy Spirit for direction. Sometimes adversity or failure is a signpost to change directions, and other times it's a marker to stay the course. We only know the difference between open and closed doors through dependency on God.

Once we begin to pursue our calling, we need to protect it. We *"live a life worthy of the calling we have received"* by guarding it with intention. Breaches in integrity not only weaken your resolve, they wreak havoc on results. God can only take you where your character can keep you. As you prioritize your life, you protect your calling. **Identify the non-negotiables by asking key questions:**

- *Am I consistently spending time in prayer and the study of God's Word?*
- *Is there a "good" I need to let go of to make room for God's "best"?*
- *What can I do that no one else can do?*
- *Where do I sense God's favor?*
- *What do I need to learn in this short season so I can sustain for the long haul?*

It's imperative to realize that a need is not a calling. I quickly became overwhelmed by the need in Africa and the complicated dynamics of establishing a sustainable ministry-business model. I fought the unwelcome emotions of inadequacy and doubt. Confusion and competition become a distraction from God's true call on our lives. Through the guidance of the Holy Spirit and strong mentors, I narrowed my focus to concentrate on pastors' wives and children in rural regions. Don't try to walk in someone else's anointing; God will uniquely use you as you follow His favor on your life. We are all *"one body...called to hope,"* accomplishing the most when we complete, not compete. Another woman's success does not diminish mine. In contrast, we encourage each other to fulfill our unique calling by sharing from our struggles along the way. If you want to experience the favor of God in your life, sow favor into the lives of others.

YOUR CATALYST FOR CHANGE—PRACTICE YOUR CALLING

"With this in mind, we constantly pray for you, that our God may make you worthy of his calling, and that by his power he may bring to fruition your every desire for goodness and your every deed prompted by faith. We pray this so that the name of our Lord Jesus may be glorified in you, and you in him, according to the grace of our God and the Lord Jesus Christ,"

(1 Thessalonians 1:11–12)

God's power *"brings to fruition your every desire for goodness and your every deed prompted by faith."* His presence brings clarity and realigns our desires with His plan. He activates the God-sized dreams planted within us for kingdom gain. We practice our purpose one God-ordained step at a time. Don't covet someone else's call and don't rush your own. Practice humility through a willingness to start small, allowing things to unfold in God's time and God's way. The above verse reminds us that the primary goal of our calling—*whatever we do*—is to bring glory to the name of Jesus Christ. Success in the kingdom of God is defined by obedience.

Priscilla's example coaches us through our tendency to compartmentalize our calling. Let your relationship with Jesus Christ permeate every aspect of your life: personal, family, ministry, and work. He guides our choices for the cause of Christ as we release every piece of real estate we own to His care. Don't let fear hold you back from knowing who you are in Christ and obeying His voice. Take your place among these astounding women of the Bible as you step into your calling. Be what He designed you to be, go where He designated you to go, and do what He destined you to do. One day, we'll meet these *"not-so-ordinary-after-all"* women of the Bible who dared to do extraordinary things. Until then, find your fearless as you let God write *your* story.

Over 100 Scriptures to Help You "Find Your Fearless"

Genesis 15:1
After this, the word of the Lord came to Abram in a vision: "Do not be afraid, Abram. I am your shield, your very great reward."

Genesis 21:17
God heard the boy crying, and the angel of God called to Hagar from heaven and said to her, "What is the matter, Hagar? Do not be afraid; God has heard the boy crying as he lies there."

Genesis 22:12
"Do not lay a hand on the boy," he said. "Do not do anything to him. Now I know that you fear God, because you have not withheld from me your son, your only son."

Genesis 26:24
That night the Lord appeared to him and said, "I am the God of your father Abraham. Do not be afraid, for I am with you; I will bless you and will increase the number of your descendants for the sake of my servant Abraham."

Genesis 42:18
On the third day, Joseph said to them, "Do this and you will live, for I fear God."

Genesis 46:3
I am God, the God of your father, he said. Do not be afraid to go down to Egypt, for I will make you into a great nation there.

Genesis 50:21
So then, don't be afraid. I will provide for you and your children. And he reassured them and spoke kindly to them.

Exodus 1:21
And because the midwives feared God, he gave them families of their own.

Exodus 14:13

Moses answered the people, "Do not be afraid. Stand firm and you will see the deliverance the Lord will bring you today. The Egyptians you see today you will never see again."

Exodus 14:31

And when the Israelites saw the mighty hand of the Lord displayed against the Egyptians, the people feared the Lord and put their trust in him and in Moses his servant.

Exodus 20:20

Moses said to the people, "Do not be afraid. God has come to test you, so that the fear of God will be with you to keep you from sinning."

Leviticus 26:6

I will grant peace in the land, and you will lie down and no one will make you afraid. I will remove wild beasts from the land, and the sword will not pass through your country.

Deuteronomy 3:22

Do not be afraid of them; the Lord your God himself will fight for you.

Deuteronomy 5:29

Oh, that their hearts would be inclined to fear me and keep all my commands always, so that it might go well with them and their children forever!

Deuteronomy 6:2

so that you, your children and their children after them may fear the Lord your God as long as you live by keeping all his decrees and commands that I give you, and so that you may enjoy long life.

Deuteronomy 6:13

Fear the Lord your God, serve him only and take your oaths in his name.

Deuteronomy 10:12

And now, Israel, what does the Lord your God ask of you but to fear the Lord your God, to walk in obedience to him, to love him, to serve the Lord your God with all your heart and with all your soul,

Deuteronomy 10:20

Fear the Lord your God and serve him. Hold fast to him and take your oaths in his name.

Deuteronomy 31:6

Be strong and courageous. Do not be afraid or terrified because of them, for the Lord your God goes with you; he will never leave you nor forsake you.

Deuteronomy 31:8

The Lord himself goes before you and will be with you; he will never leave you nor forsake you. Do not be afraid; do not be discouraged.

Deuteronomy 31:13

Their children, who do not know this law, must hear it and learn to fear the Lord your God as long as you live in the land you are crossing the Jordan to possess.

Joshua 1:9

Have I not commanded you? Be strong and courageous. Do not be afraid; do not be discouraged, for the Lord your God will be with you wherever you go.

Ruth 3:11

And now, my daughter, don't be afraid. I will do for you all you ask. All the people of my town know that you are a woman of noble character.

1 Samuel 12:14

If you fear the Lord and serve and obey him and do not rebel against his commands, and if both you and the king who reigns over you follow the Lord your God—good!

1 Samuel 12:24

But be sure to fear the Lord and serve him faithfully with all your heart; consider what great things he has done for you.

2 Samuel 9:7

Don't be afraid," David said to him, "for I will surely show you kindness for the sake of your father Jonathan. I will restore to you all the land that belonged to your grandfather Saul, and you will always eat at my table."

1 Kings 17:13

Elijah said to her, "Don't be afraid. Go home and do as you have said. But first make a small loaf of bread for me from what you have and bring it to me, and then make something for yourself and your son."

2 Kings 6:16

Don't be afraid, the prophet answered. Those who are with us are more than those who are with them.

1 Chronicles 16:25

For great is the Lord and most worthy of praise; he is to be feared above all gods.

1 Chronicles 22:13

Then you will have success if you are careful to observe the decrees and laws that the Lord gave Moses for Israel. Be strong and courageous. Do not be afraid or discouraged.

1 Chronicles 28:20

David also said to Solomon his son, "Be strong and courageous, and do the work. Do not be afraid or discouraged, for the Lord God, my God, is with you. He will not fail you or forsake you until all the work for the service of the temple of the Lord is finished."

2 Chronicles 20:15

He said: Listen, King Jehoshaphat and all who live in Judah and Jerusalem! This is what the Lord says to you: Do not be afraid or discouraged because of this vast army. For the battle is not yours, but God's.

2 Chronicles 20:17

You will not have to fight this battle. Take up your positions; stand firm and see the deliverance the Lord will give you, Judah and Jerusalem. Do not be afraid; do not be discouraged. Go out to face them tomorrow, and the Lord will be with you.

2 Chronicles 32:7

"Be strong and courageous. Do not be afraid or discouraged because of the king of Assyria and the vast army with him, for there is a greater power with us than with him."

Nehemiah 4:14

After I looked things over, I stood up and said to the nobles, the officials and the rest of the people, "Don't be afraid of them. Remember the Lord, who is great and awesome, and fight for your families, your sons and your daughters, your wives and your homes."

Job 1:8

Then the Lord said to Satan, "Have you considered my servant Job? There is no one on earth like him; he is blameless and upright, a man who fears God and shuns evil."

Job 11:19

You will lie down, with no one to make you afraid, and many will court your favor.

Psalm 3:6

I will not fear though tens of thousands assail me on every side.

Psalm 23:4

Even though I walk through the darkest valley, I will fear no evil, for you are with me; your rod and your staff, they comfort me.

Psalm 25:12

Who, then, are those who fear the Lord? He will instruct them in the ways they should choose.

Psalm 25:14

The Lord confides in those who fear him; he makes his covenant known to them.

Psalm 27:1

The Lord is my light and my salvation— whom shall I fear? The Lord is the stronghold of my life— of whom shall I be afraid?

Psalm 27:3

Though an army besiege me, my heart will not fear; though war break out against me, even then I will be confident.

Psalm 31:19

How abundant are the good things that you have stored up for those who fear you, that you bestow in the sight of all, on those who take refuge in you.

Psalm 33:8

Let all the earth fear the Lord; let all the people of the world revere him.

Psalm 33:18

But the eyes of the Lord are on those who fear him, on those whose hope is in his unfailing love,

Psalm 34:4

I sought the Lord, and he answered me; he delivered me from all my fears.

Psalm 34:7

The angel of the Lord encamps around those who fear him, and he delivers them.

Psalm 34:9

Fear the Lord, you his holy people, for those who fear him lack nothing.

Psalm 34:11

Come, my children, listen to me; I will teach you the fear of the Lord.

Psalm 46:2

Therefore, we will not fear, though the earth give way and the mountains fall into the heart of the sea,

Psalm 49:5
Why should I fear when evil days come, when wicked deceivers surround me—

Psalm 56:3
When I am afraid, I put my trust in you.

Psalm 56:4
In God, whose word I praise— In God I trust and am not afraid. What can mere mortals do to me?

Psalm 56:11
in God I trust and am not afraid. What can man do to me?

Psalm 86:11
Teach me your way, Lord, that I may rely on your faithfulness; give me an undivided heart, that I may fear your name.

Psalm 96:4
For great is the Lord and most worthy of praise; he is to be feared above all gods.

Psalm 103:13
As a father has compassion on his children, so the Lord has compassion on those who fear him;

Psalm 111:10
The fear of the Lord is the beginning of wisdom; all who follow his precepts have good understanding. To him belongs eternal praise.

Psalm 112:7
They will have no fear of bad news; their hearts are steadfast, trusting in the Lord.

Psalm 115:11
You who fear him, trust in the Lord— he is their help and shield.

Psalm 115:13

He will bless those who fear the Lord— small and great alike.

Psalm 118:4

Let those who fear the Lord say: "His love endures forever."

Psalm 118:6

The Lord is with me; I will not be afraid. What can mere mortals do to me?

Psalm 119:38

Fulfill your promise to your servant, so that you may be feared.

Psalm 119:63

I am a friend to all who fear you, to all who follow your precepts.

Psalm 119:74

May those who fear you rejoice when they see me, for I have put my hope in your word.

Psalm 139:14

I praise you because I am fearfully and wonderfully made; your works are wonderful; I know that full well.

Psalm 145:19

He fulfills the desires of those who fear him; he hears their cry and saves them.

Psalm 147:11

The Lord delights in those who fear him, who put their hope in his unfailing love.

Proverbs 1:7

The fear of the Lord is the beginning of knowledge, but fools despise wisdom and instruction.

Proverbs 1:33

"But whoever listens to me will live in safety and be at ease, without fear of harm."

Proverbs 3:7
Do not be wise in your own eyes; fear the Lord and shun evil.

Proverbs 14:26
Whoever fears the Lord has a secure fortress, and for their children it will be a refuge.

Proverbs 3:24
When you lie down, you will not be afraid; when you lie down, your sleep will be sweet.

Proverbs 14:27
The fear of the Lord is a fountain of life, turning a person from the snares of death.

Proverbs 15:16
Better a little with the fear of the Lord than great wealth with turmoil.

Proverbs 29:25
Fear of man will prove to be a snare, but whoever trusts in the Lord is kept safe.

Proverbs 31:30
Charm is deceptive, and beauty is fleeting; but a woman who fears the Lord is to be praised.

Ecclesiastes 3:14
I know that everything God does will endure forever; nothing can be added to it and nothing taken from it. God does it so that people will fear him.

Ecclesiastes 7:18
It is good to grasp the one and not let go of the other. Whoever fears God will avoid all extremes.

Isaiah 7:4
Say to him, 'Be careful, keep calm and don't be afraid. Do not lose heart because of these two smoldering stubs of firewood—because of the fierce anger of Rezin and Aram and of the son of Remaliah.'

Isaiah 12:2

"Surely God is my salvation; I will trust and not be afraid. The Lord, the Lord himself, is my strength and my defense; he has become my salvation."

Isaiah 40:9

You who bring good news to Zion, go up on a high mountain. You who bring good news to Jerusalem, lift up your voice with a shout, lift it up, do not be afraid; say to the towns of Judah, "Here is your God!"

Isaiah 41:10

So do not fear, for I am with you; do not be dismayed, for I am your God. I will strengthen you and help you; I will uphold you with my righteous right hand.

Isaiah 41:13

For I am the Lord your God who takes hold of your right hand and says to you, do not fear; I will help you.

Isaiah 43:5

Do not be afraid, for I am with you; I will bring your children from the east and gather you from the west.

Isaiah 44:8

Do not tremble, do not be afraid. Did I not proclaim this and foretell it long ago? You are my witnesses. Is there any God besides me? No, there is no other Rock; I know not one.

Isaiah 54:4

Do not be afraid; you will not be put to shame. Do not fear disgrace; you will not be humiliated. You will forget the shame of your youth and remember no more the reproach of your widowhood.

Jeremiah 1:8

"Do not be afraid of them, for I am with you and will rescue you," declares the Lord.

Jeremiah 17:8
They will be like a tree planted by the water that sends out its roots by the stream. It does not fear when heat comes; its leaves are always green. It has no worries in a year of drought and never fails to bear fruit.

Jeremiah 39:17
But I will rescue you on that day, declares the Lord; you will not be given into the hands of those you fear.

Jeremiah 51:46
Do not lose heart or be afraid when rumors are heard in the land; one rumor comes this year, another the next, rumors of violence in the land and of ruler against ruler.

Daniel 10:19
"Do not be afraid, you who are highly esteemed," he said. "Peace! Be strong now; be strong." When he spoke to me, I was strengthened and said, "Speak, my lord, since you have given me strength."

Joel 2:21
Do not be afraid, land of Judah; be glad and rejoice. Surely the Lord has done great things!

Matthew 1:20
But after he had considered this, an angel of the Lord appeared to him in a dream and said, "Joseph son of David, do not be afraid to take Mary home as your wife, because what is conceived in her is from the Holy Spirit."

Matthew 8:26
He replied, "You of little faith, why are you so afraid?" Then he got up and rebuked the winds and the waves, and it was completely calm.

Matthew 10:26
So do not be afraid of them, for there is nothing concealed that will not be disclosed, or hidden that will not be made known.

Matthew 10:28

Do not be afraid of those who kill the body but cannot kill the soul. Rather, be afraid of the One who can destroy both soul and body in hell.

Matthew 10:31

So don't be afraid; you are worth more than many sparrows.

Matthew 14:27

But Jesus immediately said to them: "Take courage! It is I. Don't be afraid."

Matthew 14:30

But when he saw the wind, he was afraid and, beginning to sink, cried out, "Lord, save me!"

Matthew 17:7

But Jesus came and touched them. "Get up," he said. "Don't be afraid."

Matthew 28:8

So the women hurried away from the tomb, afraid yet filled with joy, and ran to tell his disciples.

Matthew 28:10

Then Jesus said to them, "Do not be afraid. Go and tell my brothers to go to Galilee; there they will see me."

Mark 5:36

Overhearing what they said, Jesus told him, "Don't be afraid; just believe."

Mark 6:50

because they all saw him and were terrified. Immediately he spoke to them and said, "Take courage! It is I. Don't be afraid."

Luke 1:13

But the angel said to him: "Do not be afraid, Zechariah; your prayer has been heard. Your wife Elizabeth will bear you a son, and you are to call him John."

Luke 1:30
But the angel said to her, "Do not be afraid, Mary; you have found favor with God."

Luke 2:10
But the angel said to them, "Do not be afraid. I bring you good news that will cause great joy for all the people."

Luke 5:10
and so were James and John, the sons of Zebedee, Simon's partners. Then Jesus said to Simon, "Don't be afraid; from now on you will fish for people."

Luke 8:50
Hearing this, Jesus said to Jairus, "Don't be afraid; just believe, and she will be healed."

Luke 12:7
Indeed, the very hairs of your head are all numbered. Don't be afraid; you are worth more than many sparrows.

Luke 12:32
Do not be afraid, little flock, for your Father has been pleased to give you the kingdom.

John 6:20
But he said to them, "It is I; don't be afraid."

John 12:15
"Do not be afraid, Daughter Zion; see, your king is coming, seated on a donkey's colt."

John 14:27
Peace I leave with you; my peace I give you. I do not give to you as the world gives. Do not let your hearts be troubled and do not be afraid.

Acts 27:24
and said, 'Do not be afraid, Paul. You must stand trial before Caesar; and God has graciously given you the lives of all who sail with you.'

Ephesians 6:19

Pray also for me, that whenever I speak, words may be given me so that I will fearlessly make known the mystery of the gospel,

Hebrews 11:23

By faith Moses' parents hid him for three months after he was born, because they saw he was no ordinary child, and they were not afraid of the king's edict.

Hebrews 11:27

By faith he left Egypt, not fearing the king's anger; he persevered because he saw him who is invisible.

Hebrews 13:6

So we say with confidence, "The Lord is my helper; I will not be afraid. What can mere mortals do to me?"

1 Peter 3:14

But even if you should suffer for what is right, you are blessed. Do not fear their threats; do not be frightened.

1 John 4:18

There is no fear in love. But perfect love drives out fear, because fear has to do with punishment. The one who fears is not made perfect in love.

Revelation 1:17

When I saw him, I fell at his feet as though dead. Then he placed his right hand on me and said: "Do not be afraid. I am the First and the Last."

Revelation 2:10

Do not be afraid of what you are about to suffer. I tell you, the devil will put some of you in prison to test you, and you will suffer persecution for ten days. Be faithful, even to the point of death, and I will give you life as your victor's crown.

Revelation 19:5

Then a voice came from the throne, saying: "Praise our God, all you his servants, you who fear him, both great and small!"

Endnotes

1. Joe Parprocki, Busted Halo
2. www.gotquestions.org
3. www.workingpreacher.org
4. *All the Women of the Bible*, Herman Lockyer
5. Darby's Commentary, www.biblestudytools.com
6. The Works of Flavius Josephus
7. Barnes' Commentary, www.biblestudytools.com
8. *The Scarlet Cord of Redemption*, Carter Corbrey
9. www.guttmacher.org
10. www. RAINN.org
11. www.ProCon.org
12. www.Abort73.com
13. *All the Women of the Bible*, Herman Lockyer
14. www.biblestudytools.com
15. Matthew Henry's Commentary, www.biblestudytools.com
16. Barnes' Commentary, www.biblestudytools.com
17. Eleanor Roosevelt, www.goalcast.com
18. *Messy Grace: How a Pastor with Gay Parents Learned to Love Others Without Sacrificing Conviction*, Caleb Kaltenbach
19. Clifton Sheet, M.D.
20. Rabbi/Rev. Eric Walker, www.ignitinganation.com
21. Kim Hellemans, www.theglobeandmail.com
22. https://www.padfield.com/2005/corinth.html

ALSO AVAILABLE FROM BRIDGE-LOGOS

FINDING JOY WHEN LIFE IS OUT OF FOCUS
Angela Donadio

We all walk through seasons when joy plays an unwelcome game of hide and seek. This in-depth, verse by verse study will help you choose contentment regardless of circumstance, transform faulty thought patterns through the truth of God's Word, and persevere when life is unravelling. Filled with personal testimony and encouragement, this would be an ideal companion for groups or personal study.

Angela Donadio is an international speaker, recording artist, and advocate for deprived pastors' wives and children in Africa.

www.angeladonadio.com

ISBN: 978-1-61036-993-0

ALSO AVAILABLE FROM BRIDGE-LOGOS

ALL THE WILD PEARLS
Heather DeJesus Yates

Every pearl has a story to tell. Join lawyer, speaker and author Heather DeJesus Yates as she creatively guides our generation through the transformational hope of the Gospel using both her own redemptive stories and those of an unlikely companion...a wild oyster.

Heather DeJesus Yates is a wife, mama, business owner, speaker, blogger, occasional lawyer and legislative advocate, and author. Out of a passion to see women walk in freedom from shame, Heather woos women into God's wide love through her disarmingly real-life stories, balanced with Gospel-centered hope.

Facebook: @amotherofthousands
Instagram: @amotherofthousands
Pinterest: @amotherofthousands.
www.facebook.com/amotherofthousands
www.amotherofthousands.com

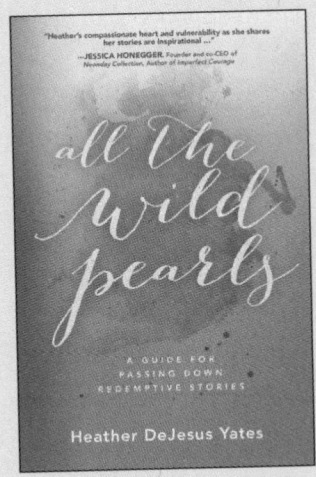

ISBN: 978-1-61036-991-6

ALSO AVAILABLE FROM BRIDGE-LOGOS

BEAUTY FROM ASHES
Donna Sparks

In a transparent and powerful manner, the author reveals how the Lord took her from the ashes of a life devastated by failed relationships and destructive behavior to bring her into a beautiful and powerful relationship with Him. The author encourages others to allow the Lord to do the same for them.

Donna Sparks is an Assemblies of God evangelist who travels widely to speak at women's conferences and retreats. She lives in Tennessee.

www.story-of-grace.com

www.facebook.com/
  donnasparksministries/

https://www.facebook.com/
  AuthorDonnaSparks/

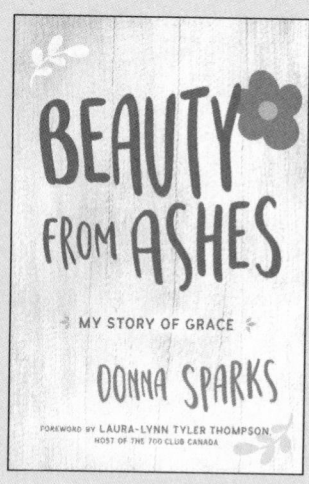

ISBN: 978-1-61036-252-8

ALSO AVAILABLE FROM BRIDGE-LOGOS

JOY FOR ALL SEASONS
Carol McLeod

Imagine reading a book that is so much more than written words on a page but, instead, an invitation to experience exuberant joy! Simply imagine the sweet hope that comes from reading about the patience, the gladness, and the excitement that is nestled within one woman's heart. Imagine! You have just imagined the devotional book entitled, "Joy for All Seasons" written by best-selling author, blogger, speaker, radio host, TV host and Bible teacher, Carol McLeod. Her capacity for joy and her resolve to trumpet the bidding to embrace joy in every week of the year is not for the faint of heart. This weekly summons into His presence is filled with rich experiences, with heart-felt celebration, and with an intimate knowledge of what it takes to walk with God.

ISBN: 9781610361965

ALSO AVAILABLE FROM BRIDGE-LOGOS

GIVING HOPE AN ADDRESS
Julie Wilkerson Klose

For sixty years, the faith-based ministry of Teen Challenge has been bringing hope to those bound by drug and life-controlling addictions. Since the very first Teen Challenge Center opened its doors in Brooklyn, New York the ministry has grown to 1,400 Centers across 122 nations.

Julie Wilkerson Klose, the daughter of Don Wilkerson and niece of David Wilkerson, grew up in the ministry of Teen Challenge. Julie is an educator and writer. She began her writing career as a regular contributor to a political website focusing on cultural issues from a Christian perspective, with a special passion for the pro-life movement.

www.JulieKlose.com

twitter@thevelvetbrick1

ISBN: 978-1-61036-472-0